Essential Communication & Influencing Skills

A Practical Guide To Verbal & Non-Verbal Communication

To My Family For All Their Love, Support, & Patience.

CONTENTS

9

OVERVIEW

How effective we are at communicating impacts how we are perceived and our life opportunities. Our ability to effectively negotiate, co-operate, and collaborate with others is increasingly important in the workplace. Skills may be trained, and experience acquired, but behaviours can be hard to change. In today's modern world, employers pay as much attention, if not more, to a candidate's ability to build strong relationships, resolve conflicts, and seek compromise, than qualifications and certifications.

As a child, I recall my grandmother saying, when she watched conflicts reported on the television, that "wars begin in the playground". I did not understand what she meant at the time. Now I realise just what a wise lady she was. Imagine a world where we all left school confident in expressing our point of view, possessed the ability to articulate our thoughts so they resonated with others and had learnt the skills to manage aggressive behaviour without being drawn into an emotional conflict.

Imagine the difference it would make if you could build strong relationships with even the most challenging of people, possessed the skills to hold difficult conversations in a way that you were understood, respected and heard, or if you could effectively influence and challenge the ideas of those around you. By the end of this book, you will have the skills and techniques to be a great communicator. You will learn:

- The science of communication. Why communication breaks down and simple techniques to ensure your message lands the way it was intended.

- How to ensure you make a great first impression in any professional or social context.

- The importance of non-verbal communication (body language) and how we can use it to influence and read others.

- Techniques for building social confidence and overcoming public speaking nerves.

- Why certain language resonates with some but not others and how to tailor your communication style to have the greatest impact.

- The power of language patterns and how to use them to build trust, project credibility, and inspire.

- Effective techniques for managing conflict and aggressive behaviour.

- The impact of group psychology and how to effectively communicate with teams and large audiences.

HOW TO GAIN THE MOST FROM THIS BOOK

This book provides the knowledge and techniques to take your communication and influencing skills to the next level. The content is deliberately structured to continually build on what you have learnt. It may also be used as a reference guide for those who wish to cherry-pick sections.

The key to mastering any skill is practice. By continually repeating any activity, over time we create new habits and behaviours. Each chapter contains exercises and self-coaching opportunities to hone your communication skills. The more you practice, the more confident and competent you will become.

I recommend that you identify a few techniques that appeal to you, or believe will have the greatest benefit and practice until you are comfortable. Then continue to add techniques to your skillset.

1

THE SCIENCE OF COMMUNICATION

"Believe nothing you hear and only one half of what you see."

Edgar Allan Poe

The vast majority of us are naturally good communicators. We frequently and successfully interact with family, friends and colleagues. Yet for all of us, there are situations where our communication lets us down. Whether that will be dealing with a challenging colleague, presenting to a room full of people, or influencing family and friends.

By having a rudimentary grasp of the science behind human communication and its inherent flaws, we are better placed to work to our strengths and avoid common pitfalls. During this chapter, we'll explore:

- How we process sensory information and why at times we can misunderstand others and be misunderstood.

- The various filters we unconsciously use to process the world around us.

- The importance of non-verbal communication or body language in determining the intended meaning behind what people say.

CAN YOU TRUST WHAT YOU SEE OR HEAR?

Our senses: sight, hearing, touch, smell, and taste are continually relaying information to our brain, which interprets the data and decides what action to take. For the most part, this process works well. Most of us have complete faith in what we see, hear and touch. I am sure we have all said or heard the phrase, 'I know what I heard' or 'I know what I saw'. However, this isn't always the case.

Until the late 1980's an eyewitness statement, placing a suspect at the scene of a crime, was one of the strongest forms of evidence that could be presented in a court of law. By the

1990's it was regarded as one of the weakest. What had changed during that time? The discovery of DNA testing highlighted a significant number of miscarriages of justice based on eyewitness testimonies. The reality is humans do not make great eyewitnesses because we do not accurately observe the world around us. Numerous subsequent studies show when a group of people witness the same crime, there are likely to be as many different accounts as there are witnesses. The accounts frequently contradict each other and are factually inaccurate.

According to the Innocence Project, as of January 2020, 367 convictions have been overturned as a result of DNA in the US since 1989. Mistaken identification by eyewitnesses (often multiple eyewitnesses) played a role in 71% of those wrongful convictions.

So why is it that people who experience the same event can have such different recollections? It all comes down to how we process sensory information.

HOW WE PROCESS SENSORY INFORMATION

Why Perception And Reality May Differ

We continually receive a huge amount of sensory information. Approximately 2 billion pieces of information per second. This is far more than our brains can handle. It is estimated that we can subconsciously process in the region of 4 million pieces of information per second and consciously between 5 and 9 pieces of information per second.

To avoid overload, our brains filter or delete approximately 80% of the information supplied by our senses. We subconsciously decide which data to delete in a split second, based on our previous experiences and what we perceive as important. (This is covered in more detail later in the section 'How We Filter The World Around Us'). Filtering or discarding data ensures we can quickly process our surroundings and the world around us. However, as a result, we have an incomplete picture of the world.

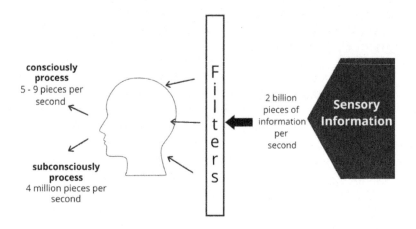

Figure 1.1

To make sense of the partial data, our brains are programmed to find meaningful patterns in the information they receive and fill in the gaps based on previous experience and the information available.

For an example of this view the text in figure 1.2. Despite some of the letters being jumbled or incorrect, we are still able to process and correctly understand the text.

> *Yuor bra1n si etxremley sophsitictaed. It cnostanlty saerch3s for pattrens in teh data ti recieves frmo teh senses adn meaks s3ns3 of 1t. Yuo cna porbalby raed tihs esaliy desptie teh msispeillgns.*
>
> *Az yoru barin d3c1ph3rs aech wrod 1t alos pr3dcits wihch wrods lgoicalyl com3 netx ot form a coher3nt setnecne.*

Figure 1.2

Physical Constraints. Filling In The Gaps

There are physical constraints that affect how we perceive the world around us which our brains resolve without us realising. For instance, our eyes are spheres. When light passes through a sphere, it inverts. This is true of light passing through our eyes.

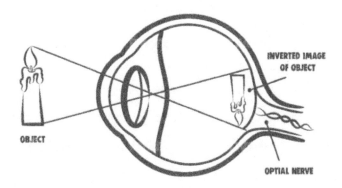

INVERTED IMAGE OF OBJECT

OBJECT

OPTIAL NERVE

Figure 1.3

19

Images projected on the retina are upside down, as illustrated in figure 1.3. Our brain automatically reverts the image, so we see it the right way up

The Blind Spot In The Middle Of Your Eye

Our eyes also contain blind spots that restrict what we see. The retina contains millions of light-sensitive cells which are sensitive to specific wavelengths of light. When they detect light, a signal is sent to the brain via the optic nerve. At the centre of the retina, where the optic nerve is attached, there are no photosensitive cells. So, our eyes cannot detect the light that lands here. This means we have a blind spot in the middle of our eyes. Yet those of us, with healthy sight, do not notice this physical constraint. This is because our brain automatically fills in the gap with what it assumes should be there (this will be covered in more detail later).

You can use the diagram in figure 1.4, and the following instructions to test the blind spot.

- Hold the diagram in front of you.

- Close your left eye and look directly at the circle on the left. You should see the circle on the right in your peripheral vision.

- Move the paper towards you whilst continuing to focus on the circle on the left.

- A point will come where the spot on the right disappears.

- Continue to move the piece of paper towards you and the spot will reappear.

- The spot disappears as it enters the blind spot created by the optic nerve.

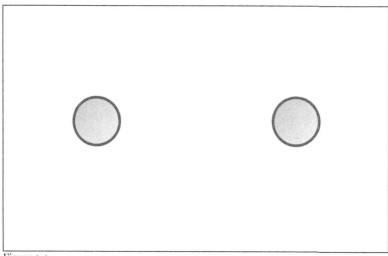

Figure 1.4

The Blind Spot At The End Of Your Nose

Receiving data from both eyes allows us to gauge depth and movement. Our brain receives slightly different information from each eye and combines it to create a single representation. When we focus on something immediately in front of us, what each eye sees can be quite different. If you place a finger immediately in front of your left eye, then, close one eye then the other in turn, you will note the view of your finger is very different. When both our eyes are open, our brain merges the two different views.

The following simple experiment illustrates this phenomenon. When we hold a tube in front of one eye then slide the other hand alongside it, there is a point along the tube where it appears to pass through the sliding hand.

- Roll a piece of A4 paper into a tube.

- Hold your left hand out flat, approximately 15 cm in front of your face.

- Hold the tube in your right hand as if it were a telescope, with the nearest point approximately 2cm in front of your eye. Take great care not to poke yourself in the eye.

- Bring your hands together in front of you so your left-hand touches the tube.

- Move the left hand along the tube towards your face. Keep both eyes open. The left hand should always be in contact with the tube. As illustrated in figures 1.5 and 1.6.

As you move your left hand along the tube there is a point where you will see a hole in your left hand that you can look through.

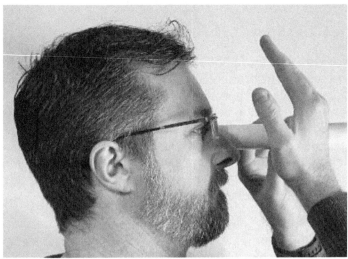

Figure 1.5

Figure 1.6

Blind Spots In Our Peripheral Vision

Like most predators, our foveal vision (what we see when we look forward and focus on something) is far more developed than our peripheral vision (what we can see at the sides of our eyes). Rather than having blurred vision, our brains fill in the gaps.

Figure 1.7 illustrates this. Count the number of dots in the grid. Do the dots appear to move?

The image contains 12 dots. When we focus directly on one section of the image, we can see the black dots in that section. The dots that are the furthest away from that section now falls within our peripheral vision. As our peripheral vision is poor and fragmented our brain fills in the gaps based on what it assumes should be there. In this case, it assumes the grey, straight lines continue without dots. It is only when we move

23

our eyes and focus on different sections of the image that the missing dots appear.

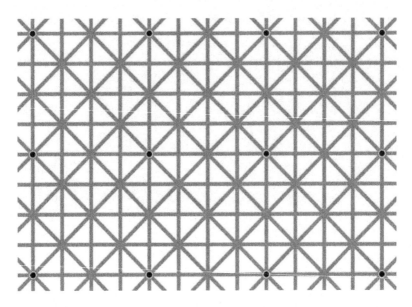

Figure 1.7

PERCEPTION AND OPTICAL ILLUSIONS

Optical illusions illustrate how our brain, whilst seeking meaning in the information it receives, can jump to the wrong conclusion. As you view the illusions over the next few pages, ask yourself again, do you believe what you see and hear?

Figure 1.8 is a well-known illusion. No doubt you see a white triangle at the centre. Although the triangle has no physical outline, we create one in our mind, as it is what we expect to see.

Figure 1.8 Kanizsa Triangle

Figure 1.9 illustrates how our mind may be tricked into miscalculating size. The vertical lines on the left are equal in length. We perceive them differently due to the fins. In a.i they add to the central shape, pulling it together. In a.ii they extend the shape, making it look bigger.

The parallel lines on the right are also the same size. The top line looks bigger because the tram lines suggest perspective and that it is further away.

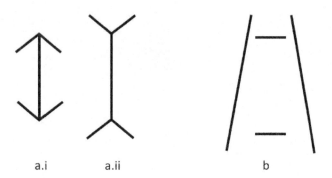

a.i a.ii   b

Figure 1.9

Figure 1.10, The Boring Figure was created by Edwin Boring in 1915. It is known as an ambiguous illusion as there are two possible interpretations. Whether we see a young or old lady depends on how our brain processes the visual information.

Figure 1.10 The Boring Figure

Once we identify a face it can be difficult to see the other, as we are only expecting one. But if you look closely, you will see the illustration contains faces.

What animal can you see in figure 1.11?

Figure 1.11 René Milot. Lion, Mouse

Do you see a lion? Turn the image 180°. Now can you see a mouse? Revert the image again and view it the correct way round. You will almost certainly be aware of both animals. As our brain initially searches for patterns, it recognises the lion and disregards the other data. We do not initially recognise the mouse because we are not accustomed to seeing a mouse upside down. When the image is rotated, we notice a recognisable pattern of a mouse. And once the image is turned the right way round, we continue to see the mouse, for we now know it is there and expect to see it.

Take a look at Figure 1.12. What do you see? If you only see a brick wall, look again.

Figure 1.12

In the centre of the wall, there is an object that we would not expect to be there. Once we see it, we are unable to not see it. Our brain recognises a pattern and deletes or ignores the rest of the information until its interpretation is challenged and consciously searches for another interpretation.

If you are still struggling to see the object, a cigar is protruding from the centre of the wall. If you are still struggling, the cigar is highlighted in an image in figure 1.14 at the end of the chapter.

What do you see in this picture? An eagle?

The eagle accounts for less than 40% of the image. 60% of the information is deleted as it is not deemed relevant.

Whenever I show this image to students on my courses, after showing them the other optical illusions, they analyse the image at length, convinced something else is hidden within it.

Figure 1.13

This again illustrates how we filter information. Recent experience leads the students to believe there must be something else in the image that they just have not seen.

Figure 1.14

How Our Hearing Can Be Tricked

It is not only our sight that can be misleading. All our senses can. Have you been to a noisy party and struggled to hear what those around you are saying? Have you noticed that after a while your hearing adjusts? It focuses on who you want to hear and starts to block out the other noise. This is referred to as the "Cocktail Effect" and was first discovered by Colin Cheery in 1953. It is the same effect when we are home alone, late at night, and we start to notice all the faint creaks and strange noises in the house. Subconsciously we hone in and amplify them.

A more recent discovery shows our mind has a built-in autocorrect. When we do not quite hear an entire sentence, our brain can fill in the gaps. When conversations were played to subjects, where background noise meant they had to strain to hear and where obvious words in some sentences were missing, frequently the subject would fill in the gaps with the appropriate word. What was interesting about this study was many subjects were unaware the words were missing. Subconsciously they had filled in the missing word or words and when asked, were unaware that the sentence had been incomplete. Have you ever had debates where you are adamant you heard one thing whilst the other person is equally adamant, they said something else? Considering our ability to subconsciously auto-correct gaps in what we hear, how certain are you now that what you heard was actually what was said?

HOW WE FILTER THE WORLD AROUND US

Our brains receive a huge amount of information every second from our senses. Far more than they can physically process. They have evolved to selectively reject most of that information. To make sense of the remaining information our brains are programmed to search for patterns in sensory data and fill in any blanks based on our experiences. Figure 1.15 illustrates the main sensory filters

Deletion - Approximately 80% of sensory data is automatically deleted, allowing us to quickly and efficiently process key information. Our brain identifies patterns in sensory data and fills in the gaps. It does this through the process of 'Distortion' and 'Generalisation'.

Distortion - Altering aspects of sensory data so it fits with what we expect.

Have you ever walked down the street and seen someone you know, but on closer inspection, you realise it isn't them? This is an example of distortion. As our brains process the fragmented information they receive, a pattern is identified. Something about the stranger walking down the street resembles a person we know. Our brain then distorts the image or fills in the gaps, so we see who we think it is. On closer inspection, when we received more complete data, we realise it is not who we thought it was.

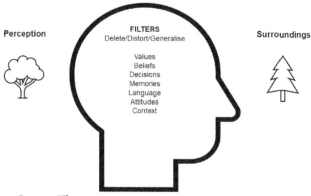

Figure 1.15 Sensory Filters

Generalisation – Drawing global conclusions based on one or two experiences.

When you see a dining room suite that looks different to yours, you do not need to be told what it is. The table and chairs have enough characteristics in common with other tables and chairs, that you know their purpose and how to use them. Our brain generalises. Rather than studying and analysing the new objects, which takes time, they are subconsciously mapped to similar objects we have encountered, and we assume they work in the same way.

Generalisation is a highly effective evolutionary strategy. Millennia ago, should one of our ancestors be attacked by a wild animal and survive, subconsciously they would record the threat. Should they encounter the same or similar creatures again, they could instinctively react, rather than wasting time consciously assessing the risk. This ability to generalise and react increased their survival chances.

Our generalisations can also negatively impact society. Subconsciously we tend to trust and connect with people who look, sound, and behave like us. We generalise based on peoples' appearances, gender and background and make assumptions based on those generalisations. These unconscious biases, that we all possess, are difficult to challenge because they are unconscious. Many organisations have championed diversity over the past few decades, yet senior leadership roles are still predominately being filled by white men.

The Filters We Use

We 'Delete', 'Distort' and 'Generalise' according to our past experiences, our memories, values and beliefs, the language we hear, our attitude, the context, and the outcome of past decisions we have made.

Values

These are things that are important to us. They are reflected in the choices we make and the things we do. We all have our own unique set of values. Their relative weighting may change depending on the context, such as, at work, at home, health and fitness or financial security.

When something is important to us, or if we find something particularly interesting, we will pay attention to it and delete other information. For example, my wife has a traditional view of children's education. She places a high value on discipline and study. In contrast, I struggled at school. I want our boys to achieve academically but it is more important to me that they are having fun and making friends. It is common for us to leave the school parents' evening with contradictory views of the discussions we had with their teachers. I focus on how they are progressing socially whilst my wife focuses more on their academic results.

Understanding another's values, what makes them tick, is key to building strong relationships and trust. (See section 'Building Trust And Rapport'). And appealing to another's values can help motivate and inspire.

Beliefs

These are the assumptions we hold true about the world. They shape what we think is and is not possible. When we hold something to be true, we will often filter out information that contradicts it, so our experiences match our beliefs. For example, many people hold a fear of public speaking. They believe they cannot do it well. Should an occasion arise when they need to speak in public, they will focus on all the aspects that could go wrong and uphold their belief. When examining the occasions they have spoken in public, they will place much greater emphasis on any errors they made above the compliments they received from their audience. Their belief they can't do it or that they are bad at it overrides the evidence at hand.

Beliefs are often irrational and can contradict logical evidence. I frequently encounter senior leaders, who even when presented with clear evidence that current working practices are less effective than their competitors, choose to reject the evidence. They believe their tried and tested ways have brought them success. They are personally invested in them.

Successfully challenging strongly held beliefs is an essential part of influencing others and ensuring they at least consider our point of view. Directly challenging beliefs is likely to reinforce them, rather than break them down. See the section on 'Meta Model – Challenging What People Think' for techniques on challenging unhelpful beliefs held by ourselves and others.

Memories And Decisions

If we have strong positive or negative recollections about an experience, we are more likely to pay attention should a similar situation occur. Someone who was laid off during an economic downturn may be more likely to tune in to the financial section of the news if they hear that the forecast is bleak.

Like many families, mine also has a few volatile relationships. I remember one Christmas taking my great Aunt to visit her sister. I was apprehensive beforehand as I knew the two did not always see eye to eye. From the moment we arrived, our host was warm and friendly and when we left, I felt that the visit had been a great success. When I returned to the car, to drive home, I noticed that my great Aunt was fuming.

"What's wrong?", I asked.

"Did you hear what she said to me?" She responded.

"When?" I asked.

"When we first arrived."

"What, Merry Christmas?", I responded puzzled.

"It's the way she said it." My great Aunt fumed.

We had both experienced the very same situation, but because we were applying different filters, that of our personal experience of the people involved, our accounts of what happened were quite different.

The success of our decisions also influences how we filter information. Particularly if the outcome was not what we intended or led to negative consequences. In that situation, we are more likely to focus on pessimistic arguments.

Language

Have you ever heard anyone describe themselves as a visual person? Or an analytical, detailed person? We all have a language preference. Some of us are visual, we prefer to see both points of view before making a decision. Whilst others are more auditory. It is all about hearing the facts. Those with a kinaesthetic preference (language dealing with feelings and sensations) want to be walked through the evidence so they can get a gut feel. Whilst an analytical person wishes to study the evidence before reaching a conclusion.

We filter sensory information based on our language preferences. If someone has a visual preference, they are more likely to notice information presented to them in a visual format. These preferences also affect the specific language that is filtered. A visual person is more likely to focus on visual language and notice sentences that contain it.

A description of how a situation looks is more likely to gain their attention than how it sounds or feels.

Understanding the language preferences of others and adapting our communication style to match theirs is an essential component of effective communication. See the section on 'Interpreting Eye Movement', for more detail on language preferences, how to use them to gain trust and increase the likelihood that our message is heard and correctly understood.

Attitudes And Opinions

These are our evaluations, positive or negative, of people, objects, events, activities, or ideas based on our past experiences. When we perceive someone or something in a positive light, we tend to accept anything positive we hear about them and reject anything less complimentary. The reverse is true when we perceive someone or something negatively.

Being aware of other people's attitudes and opinions enables us to structure our message or argument sympathetically so it is more likely to be viewed positively.

Context

Where we are, who we are with, what we are doing, all influence our perception. The Lion Mouse illusion, figure 1.11, works because we are not accustomed to the reversed image of a mouse. When we rotate the image, the mouse becomes obvious, as it appears in the context we are familiar with.

The 'The Boring Figure' illustration, figure 1.10, may be perceived in two ways. Either as a young or old lady depending upon how we process the illustration. Studies have found that when people are shown a picture of an elderly person immediately before they view the illusion, they are more likely to perceive the illustration as an elderly woman than as a young one.

THOUGHT PROCESSES AND PERCEPTION

Most of us consider ourselves rational. We consider all the arguments before reaching a logical and fair conclusion. This is often not the case in practice. Although our large brains and capability for complex thought set us apart from the rest of the animal kingdom, we use that processing power much less than we realise. During this next section, we'll examine how our thought processes impact the way we think and communicate.

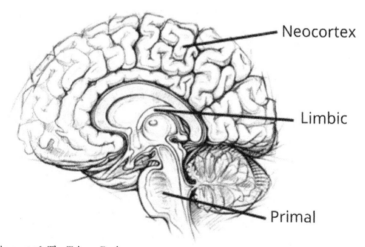

Figure 1.16 The Triune Brain

39

Intuitive Or Instinctive Thinking

The primal brain evolved over 5 million years ago. It is the oldest part of the brain and is located at the base where the brain joins the brainstem. It is also referred to as the basal ganglia, reptilian, or lizard brain. It is the home of our unconscious or instinctive thinking. It controls the body's automatic body functions such as heart rate, breathing, body temperature, blood pressure and the fight or flight response to name just a few.

It accounts for 95% of all brain activity and processes information 80, 000 times faster than the logical brain. Its primary purpose is our survival and to that end, it can override the other parts of the brain. It is the primal brain that controls our fight/flight response. When it perceives danger, it floods the body with cortisol and adrenaline. These stress hormones increase our heart and breathing rates, increasing the oxygen levels in our blood. It redirects blood flow from non-essential activities such as digestion to our muscles increasing our endurance and speed, so we are better equipped to engage the enemy or flee from it.

Intuitive or instinctive thinking has served us well as a species over the millennia. It's ensured our survival as a species. However, this safety mechanism can be counterproductive. It is these same stress hormones that cause us to panic or feel anxious before having a difficult conversation, or when we present or talk in front of others. (For information on techniques to counter the anxiety of public speaking see the section 'Overcome The Fear Of Public Speaking And Social Anxiety'). They are also produced when we feel overwhelmed, when we really focus on a task, when we are annoyed or interrupted and when we encounter hostility or aggression.

Stress hormones impact how we perceive the environment around us and how, in turn, we are perceived. With increased levels of cortisol and adrenaline in our system we are less open to new ideas, we can struggle to see the big picture, instead, getting stuck in the detail. We can also be quick to react and overreact.

Our habits or habitual behaviour are another component of our primal brain that impacts communication. Analysis and reasoning take time and energy. Our minds have evolved to identify patterns in the things we do and create instinctive or habitual responses. Often these unconscious habits are formed in our childhood, yet they continue to affect how we react to situations years later. For example, how we react to conflict and stressful situations is heavily influenced by our childhood experiences.

Emotional Thinking

The Mammalian brain or limbic system is the domain of emotional thinking. It is approximately 20 times more powerful than the logical brain and comprises of septum, amygdalae, hypothalamus, hippocampal complex, and cingulate cortex.

When we communicate on an emotional level we can inspire, motivate, and change the perceptions of others. People are more likely to buy into our arguments, and us, if they can empathise with our position. See the section on 'Intonation And Delivery' for ways to deliver emotion and energy and 'Hypnotic Language Patterns' and 'Linguistic Presuppositions For Techniques To Inspire And Motivate'.

Rational Or Logical Brain

The logical brain or neocortex is the largest part of the brain representing 85% by mass. In evolutionary terms, it is the newest. It is the reason we have made so many rapid evolutionary advances such as the development of language, and our ability to plan.

We use our logical brain far less than you may think. We simply don't have the time to analyse every piece of sensory information we receive. To win the logical argument we must first win the emotional one. See the section 'The Art Of Storytelling' for ways to bring logic to life.

OVERCOMING THE LIMITS OF OUR SENSES

This chapter has explored the science behind human communication and how we create a perception of the world around us by filtering and altering the information we receive from our senses so that the information makes sense. Because the filters we subconsciously apply are specific to our experiences, memories, beliefs, etc, so is our perception, we have a personalised view of any given situation. If we all see, hear, and feel the same situation differently, how can we be confident in our communication? How can we be sure that what we are saying is being heard and perceived the way we intended?

The remainder of this chapter explores two ways we can clarify our message and determine if it has landed correctly.

Feedback Is Key

Usually, when communicating with others we focus on ourselves and the message we are delivering rather than on our audience and how our message is being received. To be sure that our message is being interpreted correctly, feedback is key.

The Shannon-Weaver model (figure 1.17) was one of the first communication models to recognise this. It was born from the military miscommunications that occurred during the second world war in 1948. Mathematician and Electrical Engineer, Claud Shannon along with Scientist Warren Weaver explored ways of improving communication between two parties.

Their model assumes there is always the potential for communication issues (noise) between the parties (transmitter and receiver) and the way to overcome this is through feedback. What made their model different, and the reason it's still taught in human communication today, was that they placed the responsibility on the transmitter or person instigating the message to request feedback ensuring that the correct meaning of the message is received and understood.

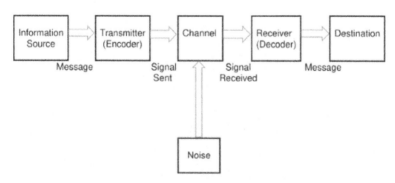

Figure 1.17 Shannon & Weaver Communication Model

In other words, the onus is on the person speaking to ensure what they are saying is understood correctly. How often is this the case when we speak to family, friends, or colleagues? How many times have you experienced or been on the receiving end of someone's frustration when you have not fully grasped what they were saying to you? How would those situations be different if the person we were speaking with took responsibility for ensuring they were understood correctly?

So how can we request feedback from those we speak with to ensure they correctly understood both the content and meaning of our message? Directly asking people to playback what we've said may work with young children, but in most situations, it's likely to cause more communication problems than it solves.

Well, there is a way that each one of us can determine how our message is landing. Through reading the other person's non-verbal communication or body language.

READING BODY LANGUAGE TO AVOID CONFUSION

When we process sensory data we create an internal representation of the world around us, how we see, hear and physically perceive the situation. Our internal representation is personal to each of us, as our filters are unique.

Each experience we have generates an emotional response. Consider your own experiences, when you visit friends, go on an exciting trip, take a relaxing holiday, or join the packed commuter train; each experience generates a different emotional response or state. This, in turn, leads to certain physiological or behavioural changes, as illustrated in figure 1.18.

For instance, consider the last relaxing holiday you enjoyed. Maybe you were laying by a pool or on the beach. Take a moment to remember that time now. Recall the sounds of the waves lapping the beach or water gurgling in the pool, the warm sun on your face. As you recall that time, the chances are you begin to feel relaxed. When we feel relaxed our physiology reflects this. Generally, our shoulders are back, and our breathing is low and slow. In contrast, when we feel nervous or tense our shoulders tend to come forward and our breathing is high and shallow. How we behave when we are relaxed also differs quite noticeably from when we are nervous or tense.

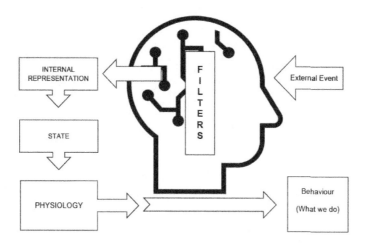

Figure 1.18

These changes in physiology and behaviour provide essential feedback on how our message has been received. In chapter 4 we'll explore non-verbal communication in more detail.

2

HOW TO MAKE A GREAT FIRST IMPRESSION

"You never get a second chance to make a first impression."

Will Rogers

First impressions are important. They set the tone for the entire relationship we have with others. They impact the degree to which people trust us, how we are judged at doing our jobs, our merit as parents, friends, and citizens. How we are placed in the social pecking order is heavily influenced by people's first impressions of us.

It is difficult to change people's perceptions once we have made a bad first impression. Behavioural research suggests it takes six positive interactions to nullify a bad first impression. So, whether you are going on a date, starting a new job, being introduced to potential in-laws, or meeting future friends it's important to get off to a good start.

THE NEUROSCIENCE OF FIRST IMPRESSIONS

When we meet someone for the first time we instinctively judge them. We analyse how they look, what they do and what they say. Subconsciously we are deciding if they are friendly and if they are someone that we'd like to engage further or if they are someone to be wary of and avoid. This evolutionary trait served us well millennia ago when the ability to quickly assess and successfully determine 'friend or foe' could mean the difference between life and death. But in modern times it can create communication barriers.

Research suggests it takes us less than a tenth of a second from meeting someone to forming an initial impression. We then spend up to a further 7 seconds looking for evidence to back up our initial judgement. After that, our first impression is fully formed.

This subconscious processing is the reason many of us struggle to remember names when we first meet someone. We are so preoccupied with assessing them and their threat level that we either don't pay attention to their name or we don't record it to memory. We'll cover this in more detail later, along with memory techniques to help us remember names.

When we first meet people we subconsciously place them into one of four categories: like/trustworthy; dislike/threat; potential sexual partner; or indifference.

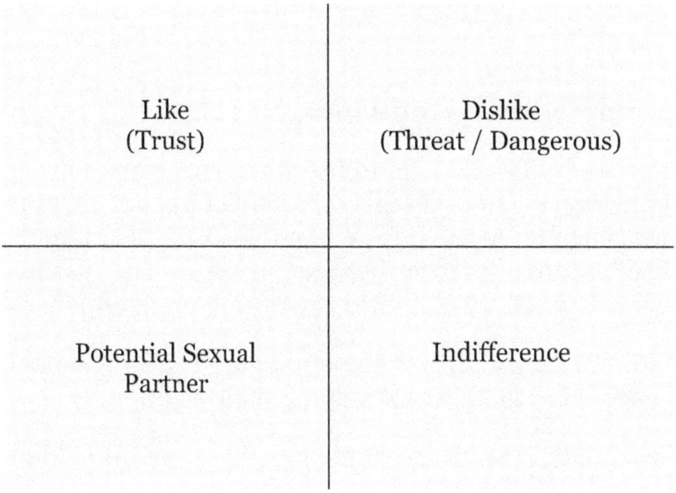

Like (Trust)	Dislike (Threat / Dangerous)
Potential Sexual Partner	Indifference

Figure 2.0

To be an effective communicator and positively influence others, we must be viewed within the 'Like/Trust' category. Yet we instinctively categorise the majority of people we meet with 'Indifference'.

There are simple nonverbal communication techniques we can use that will increase the likelihood of us being perceived positively and therefore that the message we communicate will land well. These are discussed in the next section.

INFLUENCE THROUGH BODY LANGUAGE

When we first meet someone, our initial judgement is based mostly on their appearance and how they sound. We pay little attention to what they say. There are certain physical characteristics or body language we either instinctively warm to or that trigger alarms. By understanding these characteristics, we can consciously adopt the correct ones to ensure we are perceived in a positive light by those we meet.

Manipulation Vs Influence

Often when I teach communication courses and particularly when covering non-verbal communication, delegates raise the question of manipulation. When they do, I ask them to consider the differences between influence and manipulation. Over the years, the definitions we have landed upon are:

Influence: The ability to change someone else's perspective or to encourage them to re-evaluate their position.

Manipulate: Encourage someone to do something, that is not in their best interest.

When we influence, there is no hidden or negative agenda. The intention of my communication workshops, and indeed this book, is to help people improve their communication and influencing skills. It is up to the delegates and readers how they choose to use those skills.

To those who plan to manipulate, it may gain you some short-term success but at a long-term expense. We are all natural experts at reading body language. The chances are, rather than manipulating, you'll merely break rapport and reduce your ability to influence.

Confidence And Credibility

The way we stand, walk and sit projects information about us. Walking tall or standing, with feet shoulder-width apart, keeping our back straight, shoulders back and chin up, as illustrated in figure 2.1, projects credibility, authority, and confidence.

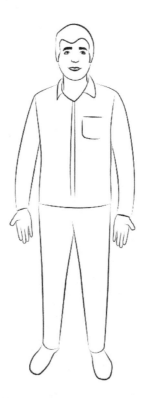

Figure 2.1 Confidence and authoritative physiology

In contrast, sitting, standing or walking with our head down, shoulders forward and back hunched, as illustrated in figure 2.2 may give the impression we lack confidence, are timid or have low ambition.

Figure 2.2 Anxious physiology

By being mindful of our physiology and when necessary, making a few simple corrections we can make a profound difference in how we are perceived, whether entering a room, making a point in a meeting, or being introduced to someone for the first time, adopting a confident, authoritative posture is likely to project that image to our audience.

Approachable And Friendly

Certain physiology projects likeability and approachability. **Smiling** is one of the simplest and most effective things we can do to put people at ease and reduce hostility from others. It suggests, at a subconscious level that we are not a threat. It can be combined with 'creditable' physiology to ensure we are not perceived as aggressive or arrogant. Combining smiling with the occasional **eyebrow** raise further conveys friendship. Eyebrow raise is a universal acknowledgement of acceptance.

Figure 2.3 Casual, friendly stance

Standing confidently with one foot in front of the other in an L shape, as illustrated in figure 2.3 also projects friendliness and approachability. It is the physiology we commonly adopt when socialising with friends. Other examples of friendly physiology include leaning against something such as a wall or having one or both hands in our pockets. When we feel socially nervous or awkward we may instinctively adopt approachable or friendly physiology as it encourages others to perceive us as non-threatening. But this can be at a cost.

We tend to subconsciously associate people demonstrating friendly, non-threatening physiology as lacking authority and credibility. If we are in an environment where being perceived as credible and authoritative is important, such as meeting work colleagues, clients or even potential in-laws, checking and correcting our default physiology could be the thing that ensures a great first impression.

Charisma - Credibility Vs Likability

Consider the leaders you know. Whether they are politicians, world states-people, or a former boss. The ones who project authority and credibility are not necessarily the ones that we most warm to. Often there is a trade-off between the two; we do not always view nice people as being great leaders. How we are perceived is less about what we say and more about how we say it. Most of us do not have a personal relationship with our politicians, yet we warm to some and not others. Our perception of them is based mainly on their non-verbal communication.

The leaders with the greatest influence are those who are both likeable and credible. We follow them because what they say resonates both logically and emotionally. When people project both likability and credibility they are referred to as **charismatic**. When I think of charismatic world leaders, Barack Obama springs to mind. Putting political views to one side, most people would consider the former President to be both likeable and credible.

Most of us do not possess natural charisma. We tend to fall into one of the two categories, likeable or credible. By understanding the subconscious impact our physiology has on others and being aware of our posture, we can modify it to achieve the best results. Adopting approachable or friendly physiology when we want to put people at ease and confident and authoritative physiology when we want to make an impact.

Inclusive Vs Directive – It's In The Hands

Holding our hands out with our palms facing up, as illustrated in figure 2.4 projects friendliness. It is perceived as welcoming and inclusive. Whilst holding our hands out, with palms facing down, as illustrated in figure 2.5, projects authority.

Figure 2.4 Hands up, inclusive gesture

Figure 2.5 Hands down, instruction.

When talking with others, palms up is a great way to request feedback and collaboration, encourage people to consider our ideas and invite support. Subconsciously, it says, I'm one of you. We're all in this together.

The hand or hands-down gesture is an effective way of injecting authority and invoking compliance. People are more likely to accept the point we are making or our instruction when they see this pose. Take care though, overusing this gesture can lead to us being perceived as bossy or authoritarian.

Exercise:

If you'd like an illustration of just how effective changing physiology can be, try the following.

Say a phrase, with your arms open and palms up. Then turn your palms so they face down and repeat the phrase. Notice how different the two phrases sound.

Physiology To Avoid

Certain physiology and behaviours are likely to portray us in a negative light.

Hostile Or Defensive Physiology

When we feel threatened or anxious, we instinctively adopt certain physiology:

- We cover our torso with our arms to protect our vital organs.
- We lower our chins to protect our vulnerable necks.
- We avoid prolonged eye contact.

When we view others demonstrating these behaviours we may subconsciously and incorrectly perceive them as hostile. When we fold our arms, whether intentional or not, we are demonstrating potentially hostile physiology.

Many of us fold our arms without any hostile or aggressive intent. Often because it just feels comfortable. Nevertheless, if we fold our arms whilst listening to someone, or in the presence of someone we've just met, there's a danger we'll be perceived as uninterested in them, hostile to their point of view. Other physiology that has a similar, subconscious effect is clenching our fists, muscle flexing and squinting.

The Awkward Handshake

A handshake is an important social interaction within western cultures. It dates back to the middle-ages, when approaching someone with our right hand out and open conveyed peaceful intent. Traditionally it was the right hand that was used for sword fighting.

There is no right answer to what makes a perfect handshake. People's preferences differ. There is pretty much universal agreement that an overly firm handshake, having your hand crushed, is not pleasant. At the other extreme, limp handshakes also create a negative first impression. So do handshakes that seem to go on for an eternity. What is deemed too strong, too soft, or too long is subjective. People don't knowingly offer a limp, overly strong (with a few exceptions) or overly long handshake. If you've never sought feedback, how do you know that your handshake doesn't fall into one of those categories?

One of the things I do when training new consultants is to ask them to shake hands with each other and provide feedback. If you are unsure how your handshake is perceived, you may want to do likewise with a friend.

Practical Example

A few years ago, I attended a conference where a speaker delivered an excellent presentation that was warmly received by the 50 or so delegates. Towards the end of his presentation, the speaker asked for a volunteer to join him on stage. The hall was silent. Other presentations at the same conference had also asked for volunteers which had resulted in many hands in the air. However, the same request here had resulted in uncomfortable silence. The speaker had then asked all of us to look under our chairs. Under one chair he had stuck a ticket and the person who's chair it was reluctantly walked to the stage.

When I spoke with the speaker after the talk, he explained he always struggled to attract volunteers. The ticket under the chair tactic was the only way he could achieve it. Despite being incredibly experienced, knowledgeable, and engaging he could not persuade delegates onto the stage as other speakers could. I have no doubt this was due to his non-verbal communication. At over 6 ft tall and with a broad frame, he was already physically imposing. Throughout his talk, he kept his arms close to his chest (which can be perceived as aggressive or defensive behaviour). When he made key points or asked questions, he pointed to the audience with his index finger, his other fingers forming a closed fist, facing down (credible and authoritative behaviour). It resembled a boxer throwing a jab. And when he made his points or drew conclusions, he used phrases such as 'You must' and 'You need to'. Throughout the entire 45-minute talk I do not believe I saw him smile once.

Had he adopted more 'friendly' body language and inclusive phrases I am certain many delegates would have volunteered to work with him.

Be Perceived As A Good listener

We all appreciate being listened to whilst we share our ideas, thoughts, and experiences, don't we? And there is nothing more certain to break rapport than looking disinterested or unengaged whilst someone else is talking. There are a few simple techniques that convey deep listening. Without a doubt, the most effective way to be perceived as tentatively listening is to actually listen. We are all naturally good at reading people. When we are not fully listening, it is obvious to the other party. Physiology that projects tentative listening includes touching one's chin, nodding, and occasionally looking up whilst considering points. We will cover listening skills in more detail in Chapter 4.

How To Tell If It's Working

There are a few tell-tale signs we can look for when talking to individuals or groups to determine if our audience are positively engaged:

- **Nods** and **Smiles**: When your audience smiles and nods, it is a sign you have built rapport (you have gained their trust). A way to test this is to smile and nod whilst talking and note who responds in kind.

- **Laughter** (in the right places): Smiling and laughter at jokes is a good indication that your audience has bought into you.

- **Open Body Language**: Arms by the side of the body rather than folded in front of the body can indicate that you are being perceived well. (Closed body language, such as arms folded and frowning, maybe a sign to change tact).

THE POWER OF NAMES

"A person's name is to that person, the sweetest, most important sound in any language."

Dale Carnegie

How do you feel when people you have only recently met remember your name and what you do? Remembering and using a person's name has a powerful impact. It demonstrates respect and naturally builds rapport.

We all respond positively to our name. We've been programmed to since the moment we were born. When we refer to someone by name, they are more attentive to what we say.

How about if someone not only remembers your name but that of your partner or the topics you discussed the last time you met? Remembering names and facts about people is an incredibly powerful way to make a positive impression.

Most people that I have met claim they are terrible at remembering names. As explained at the start of the chapter, when we meet people for the first time our subconscious mind is actively focused on assessing any potential threat the stranger may pose. As a result, it is both natural and common to pay less attention to the names that are spoken. This occurs for all of us. When we forget the person's name to whom we have just been introduced, the chances are they have forgotten ours too. Yet how often do we muddle along, hoping they will not realise or even worse, fear we may be asked to introduce them to someone else.

Simply acknowledging we cannot recall their name, and asking if they could repeat it, actually demonstrates confidence. At the same time repeating our name may well put them at ease should they also have forgotten it. I use this tactic frequently when networking and running training events. No one has ever taken offence. On the contrary, it tends to put people at ease.

On a few occasions, when I have started to reintroduce myself, they have beaten me to it and stated my name. Rather than taking this as a reflection on my poor memory, I take it as a compliment. I must have made a good first impression. I will then compliment my new friend on having a great memory, as we all enjoy a compliment.

MEMORY TECHNIQUES

The following are simple techniques that can help us recall the names and facts about the people we meet.

Remember Through Association

An effective technique for remembering names is to associate them with something meaningful or amusing. Try splitting the name into syllables, with an image for each, that tell a story. Visualise the pictures. The more humorous or absurd the image, the more likely we are to remember it.

For Example:

To recall 'Angela Macleod', picture '*Angelina Jolie, wearing a rain mac whilst standing under a dark cloud as the rain pours down*'.

If you have a particularly challenging name to remember or pronounce it is a good idea to create a humorous description you can share with people to help them remember it. This will make them feel less uncomfortable should they be struggling.

A few years ago, I worked with a Portuguese man, Santiago Catarino. I really struggled to remember his name. Partly due to the speed with which he said it but also because the sounds were new to me. He noticed me struggling and was prepared. He said, "*imagine I'm St Santiago. See the glowing halo above my head. Next to me is a rhinoceros with a cat on its back. Santiago Cat-on-a-rhino.*" With this image in my head, I never forgot his name again.

Repetition

Repetition is a key element of memory. The more often we hear something, the more likely we are to remember it. Repeating someone's name in your head when you first hear it helps the memory process it. So, does using their name early in the conversation and frequently throughout.

Keep Notes

I have worked as a consultant for many years, during which time I met numerous clients. I kept a journal in which I wrote down facts about them such as their partner's and children's names, their interests outside of work and holiday plans. I would review the journal just before I met with them. The ability to recall a story they once shared, where they went on holiday; or asking how their son got on at the county championship, helped build and maintain a strong relationship.

PROMOTE YOURSELF WITH CONFIDENCE

How comfortable are you talking about yourself? Can you confidently describe who you are and what you do? For most of us, this is a challenge. Describing ourselves or promoting what we do can make many of us feel uncomfortable. This discomfort is evident in our body language, tone of voice, and facial expressions.

Preparing a short elevator pitch, a 90-second description of ourselves (approximately the same amount of time we could spend with someone in an elevator, travelling between floors) and rehearsing it until we feel confident can help project both confidence and credibility when we deliver it.

A great way to improve our delivery is to record it on a phone or similar device and play it back. You will likely notice traits and behaviours you were previously unaware of. Such as how many times you say 'erm' or distracting hand gestures. Once aware of these traits we can change them. Instinctively we will correct the behaviours that do not look right to us. Try this a few times and notice the difference it makes.

QUICKLY BUILD TRUST AND RAPPORT

"Rapport - A close and harmonious relationship in which the people or groups concerned understand each other's feelings or ideas and communicate well."

Oxford Languages

Rapport is a term used when we feel comfortable or at ease with others. Have you ever looked around a busy restaurant and noticed how some couples seem really connected? They appear to mirror each other. When one moves an arm the other instinctively follows. Or have you noticed how people who know each other well may finish each other's sentences? They anticipate what the other will say.

When we build rapport, we are building mutual trust and respect. It is a key component of effective communication. When we are in rapport with someone, we are more likely to listen to them and take on board their point of view. So, consider how useful it would be to have the ability to create strong rapport with someone before sharing your opinion or asking for their support.

This section covers how we can identify when we have rapport with others, and the techniques to build it.

What Is Rapport

When we have rapport with others we tend to copy or mimic their physiology. This is done in one of three ways.

Matching

Copying all or part of another person's physiology. (When one person raises their left hand, the other person follows). As illustrated in Figure 2.6.

Mirroring

Mirroring all or part of another person's physiology. (When one person raises their left hand, the other person raises their right as if looking in a mirror). As illustrated in Figure 2.7.

Figure 2.6 The two characters are matching each other.

Figure 2.7 The two characters are a mirror image of each other

Cross-Over Matching

This is where one person mirrors or matches the physiology of another but using a different part of their body. For example, one person crossing their arms and the other their legs. Or matching someone's breathing rhythm with a hand movement.

Exercise

The next time you are in a public space, such as on public transport, in a park, shopping centre or restaurant, spend a few minutes people-watching. *Pay particular attention to couples and groups.*

Assess from their body language whether or not they have rapport. Are they mirroring, matching or cross over matching each other? See if you can identify those with good rapport and those who do not get on well.

Effective Ways To Quickly Build Rapport

When we communicate with our audience whilst not in rapport, our message may either be ignored or viewed with suspicion. Being able to identify when we are in rapport with others enables us to time the delivery of our key points, so they have the biggest impact.

We can build deep rapport or trust with others through our physiology and the language we use. We subconsciously trust people who look, behave and sound like us. Altering our physiology, matching, mirroring, or cross-over matching) another's behaviours or gestures subconsciously builds rapport. Adopting similar language, using the same words, tone of voice, phrases, and verbal labels as the person we are talking to, builds trust on a subconscious level. This is covered in more detail in the section 'Understanding Your Preferred Communication Style'.

Testing Rapport - Pacing And Leading

Pacing and leading is a simple way to build and test rapport with others. The process is as follows.

Exercise

- *Observe the person/people you are with. Notice their behaviours, mannerism, hand gestures, and physiology.*

- *Follow or 'Pace' them by matching, mirroring or cross over matching their movements. If they are tapping their finger, tap yours, or if they are leaning in towards you, do likewise. If they fold their arms, fold yours. (If you are in a group, focus on the most dominant or influential person in the group. The others are likely to follow that person).*

- *After 'Pacing' the other person for a while, test to see if you have built rapport by 'Leading'. Make a subtle, movement of your own. Maybe move or cross your arms, lean forward or back. If the other person responds by making the same or similar movement, you have achieved rapport. If they do not, continue pacing. The rule is to 'Pace' the other person's behaviours at least three times, then inject a behaviour of your own 'Lead'.*

Lead to A Calmer Place

Have you witnessed what happens when someone who is irate and angry is asked to calm down? The chances are it had the opposite effect. When we are annoyed and animated, being confronted by someone calm, considered, and slow-moving breaks rapport. We can feel that our view is not being taken seriously. Those trained in conflict resolution do not make this mistake. They are trained to 'Pace' to establish rapport, then 'Lead' to a calmer place. When confronted with anger, they will mirror that behaviour, though at a lower intensity. This may mean talking quickly with a raised voice and gesticulating. Once they have paced for a while, they will gradually lead the person to a calmer state. Lowering their voice and slowing the speed of their speech and movements.

I was asked to coach a team that was perceived as failing by their manager. There was a lot of bad feeling between both parties which boiled over at the introductory meeting. I was introduced by the manager as the person who would finally cut through their excuses and get them working. Instantly, the team's body language changed. One member physically turned away from me and started texting on his phone (clearly stating where he thought I could go). Another became incredibly animated as he defended his position and the team's. He spoke so quickly I struggled to follow what he was saying, and his arms flew around at the same speed. As a team coach, this was pretty much the worst start I could have with a team. So, I decided to use the 'Pace, Lead' model to build rapport.

When the animated chap paused for breath, I asked the team what their biggest challenge was. The leader said: "We have no idea what the business wants from us". I responded by banging my hand on the desk, to get their attention. Then mirroring the gesticulator, I waved my hands in the air and stated, "So you've no chance then!" I then turned my body away from the group to mirror the most extreme reaction I was seeing from them. I continued to gesticulate as I explained that without direction, they were set up to fail. Gradually I slowed the speed of my voice and hand gestures, and I began turning to face the team. They mirrored my actions and slowly turned towards me. Five minutes later we were having a calm conversation about how we should proceed.

Build Rapport By Matching Values And Interest

The strongest way to build rapport is by matching the other person's values and interests. If we understand what is important to another person and can demonstrate we have the same values or interests, we create a strong bond with that person. Children are an obvious example. For those of us who are parents, children tend to be a significant part of our lives. So, parents automatically have a common bond. Other common examples include sports, hobbies, and television programmes.

A colleague of mine some years ago really struggled with the CTO of an organisation we were working with. Whilst I had a particularly good relationship with him. My colleague was offloading to me one day, saying that no matter what he did, this prickly character just would not give him a chance and at times was downright rude. He asked how I managed to work with him. My answer was 'cricket'. We had a shared love of the game, which meant we had common ground. I would ask him his opinions on the upcoming tests series and who he would pick to play. Through this we quickly built rapport. Only when we had rapport did I then start having more challenging conversations relating to work.

My colleague was a bigger cricket fan than me, so he followed my approach. Whenever he bumped into the CTO in the office, he would spark up a cricket-related conversation. Rapidly their relationship improved. Although they did not always see eye to eye, the CTO's abrupt behaviour and negative comments towards my colleague stopped.

How To Become A Good Conversationalist

The ability to strike up an engaging conversation will not only ensure we are remembered, it also builds trust. For many, the thought of speaking with strangers can be daunting. What to say or not to say. What if the conversation dries up? The following are characteristics generally associated with good conversationalists, along with a few tips that can ease anxiety and improve small talk:

Be A Good Listener

"One of the most sincere forms of respect is actually listening to what another has to say."

Bryant H. McGill

To what degree, when engaged in a conversation are you truly listening to the other person? Often, we focus more on what we wish to say than on what is currently being said. By actively listening and being curious we make others feel valued and discover more about them. (We will cover listening skills in more detail in Chapter 4).

Be Genuinely Interested

"Everyone you will ever meet knows something you don't."

Bill Nye

It is obvious from what we say and our body language when we have a genuine interest in other people. By asking purposeful questions, encouraging the other person to talk about themselves and being curious about their answers, we build strong rapport and make a lasting impression.

Asking open-ended questions empowers those we are speaking with to take the conversation in the direction they want to, so we are far more likely to discover a person's interests and experiences if we give them control. Ask questions that begin with why, what, where, how and when, then ask follow-up questions to their answers.

Positivity

"Send out a cheerful, positive greeting, and most of the time you will get back a cheerful, positive greeting. It's also true that if you send out a negative greeting, you will, in most cases, get back a negative greeting."

Zig Ziglar

Choose positive and meaningful topics over negative ones. If the coffee at the venue is awful, why mention it? By being positive, people will in turn feel positive after meeting and talking with you.

Avoid Arguments

"The only way to get the best of an argument is to avoid it"

Dale Carnegie

Where there are differences, agree to disagree. What does winning an argument achieve if it damages the relationship? When we respect each other's point of view we can learn a lot about each other. We may also learn something about ourselves.

Put Others In Their Best Light

"How you make others feel about themselves says a lot about you"

Unknown

It is easy to downplay our own achievements. Most of us feel uncomfortable promoting our successes. So, recognising and acknowledging the achievements of others is likely to have a positive effect on that person and leave a lasting impression.

Embrace Differences

"It is not our differences that divide us, it is our inability to recognize, accept and celebrate those differences"

Audre Lorde

We are all different, the world would be a dull place if this were not true. People can say the strangest things, particularly when nervous or experiencing discomfort. If we give people a chance, they may surprise us.

Be Confident And Authentic

"No legacy is so rich as honesty"

Shakespeare

Often, when in unfamiliar social settings, we can hold back from being our true selves. This can be for many reasons, fear of being judged, social anxiety, lack of confidence. Holding back is a natural protection mechanism that others pick up on. We may come across as being disingenuous or closed. Being authentic and having the courage to show vulnerability builds trust in others and helps encourage them to open up.

3

OVERCOME THE FEAR OF PUBLIC SPEAKING

"Tell your truth, find your voice, sing your song."

Unknown

Are you one of the many people who are terrified at the thought of public speaking? Glossophobia or the fear of public speaking affects as many as 7 in 10 of us to some degree. As well as the emotional and physical discomfort it causes, it can limit career opportunities because the most articulate and confident speakers are presumed to be the most capable employees.

This chapter explores why so many of us fear public speaking or suffer from social anxiety and it provides practical tips and techniques to help us overcome these fears and deliver our message with confidence.

WHY SO MANY FEAR PUBLIC SPEAKING

There are many reasons why people fear speaking in public. The following are just a few of the reasons I've been given by clients over the years. All of which we have successfully challenged.

- I've nothing to say or no one wants to listen to me.
- I'm not interesting.
- I can't do small talk.
- I'll make a fool of myself or say something stupid.
- Speaking in public terrifies me.
- I hate being the centre of attention.
- I can't speak when lots of people are staring at me.
- What if I'm asked a question I can't answer?
- What if I forget my words?
- I panic and can't get my words out.

- I may get stuck with someone and get away without being rude.

Psychologists believe we are born with only two fears, loud noises and falling. That all other fears and phobias are learnt behaviours. We have only to watch young children for a short time this is true. Being vocal and expressing themselves is rarely a challenge for a toddler. Yet by adulthood for many, this has changed. The specific cause will vary but the process is the same.

Our brains are programmed to protect us. When we experience danger the 'fight or flight' response is triggered, and adrenaline and cortisol are released into the bloodstream. These stress hormones cause our body to undergo physiological changes. Our heart rate, blood pressure and breathing rate increase to provide the energy and oxygen we may need to rapidly respond to the danger. Blood is diverted from major organs such as the stomach to our muscles. This is why we may feel nauseous when we feel stressed or anxious. When facing imminent danger, digesting food is not a priority, being able to run faster and for longer is. These changes ensure we are at our peak physical condition to meet the threat.

We subconsciously remember danger so if we encounter it again we can react instinctively. This is a successful evolutionary strategy. The ability to quickly react to danger provided our ancestors with precious seconds that could be the difference between life and death. It is this same process behind our fear of public speaking. At some point in our lives, we experienced a scary event. Maybe being forced to stand at the front of the class and read out loud from a book whilst at school or being asked a question and feeling ridiculed for not knowing the answer. Should we then experience a similar situation, such as speaking in public, we subconsciously register danger.

The body's' fight or flight' response is extremely unhelpful for communication. Elevated heart and breathing rates make speech more difficult, as it leaves us breathless. The redirection of blood from the major organs to our muscles can leave us feeling nauseous and for many, our faces and neck turn a bright shade of pink. All of which occurs in front of our audience, increasing our stress levels, reinforcing the subconscious association between public speaking and danger.

The great thing for those who experience these fears is that it need not be this way. Just as these behaviours are learnt, they can be unlearnt.

BREAKING THE WORRY CYCLE

Worrying about upcoming events reinforces our fear of them, which in turn leads to more worry. It also increases the stress hormones in our system and our ability to rationally process stress triggers. As described in figure 3.0.

Trigger – This could be being asked to present at the next company away day, leading to negative thinking about what might happen.

Thoughts – We start to imagine the event in a negative light. What might go wrong, all the people who'll be there to see it. How we will be perceived etc.

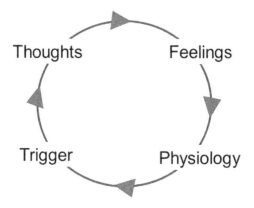

Figure 3.0 The anxiety cycle.

Feelings – These negative thoughts can be terrifying. The more we dwell on them, the more intense the feelings become.

Physiology – Anxious feelings have a physiological impact. Loss of appetite or nauseousness, muscle tension, headaches, insomnia. The more this builds, the more we focus on the trigger and the upcoming event. Which perpetuates the worry cycle.

Without exception, everyone I have spoken to who dreads speaking in public agrees that the actual event was never as bad as they feared it would be. Many even admit to enjoying it once they've started. By breaking the worry cycle, we can reduce our stress levels and change our perception of our fear. The remainder of this chapter focuses on practical techniques for breaking the anxiety cycle and building confidence.

BUILD CONFIDENCE AND OVERCOME ANXIETY

Create A Positive Mindset

How often are we our own worst critic, focusing on the tiniest flaw or imagining the worst-case scenario? The following are simple techniques that can help all of us challenge this negative thinking and create a positive mindset.

Distraction

Whilst our mind is occupied it hasn't the capacity for worry. When we feel the nerves building, do something positive. Go for a walk, read a book, watch a comedy, exercise, or try some of the techniques below.

Change Your Physiology, Change How You Feel

I explained in the earlier section how our 'fight-flight' response to danger results in instinctive physiological changes. When we are anxious or stressed, we subconsciously adopt a defensive posture.

Just as our brain chemistry directly impacts our physiology, our physiology can also impact our brain chemistry. Studies show when people who do not experience anxiety, mimic the physical characteristics of it, (chin down, shoulders forward, arms across the chest and short, shallow breathing), their levels of cortisol and adrenalin increase. Whilst mimicking the physiology of someone with confidence (shoulders back, feet apart, chin up with low deep breathing) reduces stress chemicals and increases the levels of serotonin; a chemical that makes us feel happy. Thus, by taking on the physical characteristics of confidence, we can trick our brains into producing the necessary brain chemistry, so we feel confident.

"Fake it till you make it"

Amy Cuddy

So, should you find yourself feeling anxious when a calm, confidence would be more helpful, pretend you are confident and you are likely to begin feeling that way.

For most people, confidence is associated with the following physiology:

- Back straight, shoulders back and feet shoulder-width apart.
- Head up.
- Arms held out or by the side of the body (not held in front of the body).

Imagine what it was like the last time you really felt confident. Take on the same posture now. Hold it for a minute and notice the difference it makes. The next time you find yourself feeling anxious, note your physiology. The chances are you will have adopted the anxious physical characteristics described previously. Instead, adopt the characteristics of confidence and notice the difference it makes.

Other physiology known to positively impact brain chemistry includes:

Smiling – When we smile, we automatically feel happy. Try it and see.

Low Deep Breathing – Quick, short shallow breaths are associated with stress or anxiety. Low deep breathing, exhaling for twice as long as inhaling, has a calming effect.

Looking Up - Where we look can make a difference. Are you familiar with the phrase downright angry? Approximately 80% of us, when we experience strong emotions, look down and to the right, whilst 20% down to the left. By simply looking up we can decrease the intensity of the emotion we are experiencing.

Challenge Negative Thinking

We tend to be our own worst critics, focussing on all the things that could go wrong. This can be beneficial to some degree as it can motivate us and help us avoid potential pitfalls. However, obsessing over the negatives and actively imagining all the things that could go wrong adds to the stress cycle. By challenging our inner voice or thought processes we can reprogram them to be more constructive. The following are simple ways to challenge our negative thinking.

Objectively Scrutinise The Evidence

Often our concerns defy logic. We focus on scenarios that are extreme and unlikely to happen. When you find yourself doing this, ask yourself how likely is it to occur? And what would happen if it did? Often our worst-case scenario isn't so bad.

Get A Second Opinion

We can struggle to be rational and objective when analysing our fears. Try viewing them from a different perspective. Ask a trusted friend or imagine what they would say if you shared your concerns.

Silence The Inner Critic

When you find your thoughts telling you that 'it will be terrible' or that 'you cannot do it', play those thoughts back to yourself but apply a comical voice. Maybe Donald Duck or a politician who you don't trust. If you can't take their suggestions seriously you'll stop believing them.

Visualise Success

This is a technique used by professional athletes and public speakers to build confidence and motivation. Our subconscious cannot distinguish between fact and imagination. By visualising success, we start to believe it is possible. Imagine the future event that concerns you being incredibly successful. Visualise it as if you were there, see it through your own eyes. Notice people's reactions, and how good you feel. By doing this each time we feel anxious about an event, we will change our subconscious perception.

CALM YOUR THOUGHTS WITH PERIPHERAL VISION

When we experience danger it is our sympathetic nervous system that triggers the 'fight or flight' response. It increases the production of stress hormones and releases them into the bloodstream. Our parasympathetic nervous system has a calming effect on the body. It is responsible for digestion and preparing us for sleep. It lowers our heart rate and neutralises the stress hormones once the perceived danger has passed.

The sympathetic nervous system is associated with foveal vision, directly focusing on an object. When we encounter a threat we solely focus on it. Whilst the parasympathetic nervous system is associated with peripheral vision. Being aware of everything around us. If you think about the last time you felt really relaxed, maybe laying by the pool or at the beach whilst on holiday. The chances are you weren't focused on any one thing but were absorbing everything around you.

Simply switching from foveal to peripheral vision when we feel anxious or stressed, activates the parasympathetic nervous system. As the two nervous systems cannot be active at the same time, the body will naturally calm. This is incredibly simple to do. Step by step instructions are provided below.

1. Focus on an object in front of you.

2. Notice more and more what is to each side and above the object, whilst always watching the object.

3. Raise your hands out to the sides and move them back until you can no longer just see them. Then bring them forwards until they are just in range. You may find it helpful to wiggle your fingers as peripheral vision is sensitive to movement.

4. Slowly keep moving your hands backwards until you can no longer see them and then bring them forward until they are just in range. As your mind adjusts to peripheral vision you'll notice that you can see further and further back. You may also notice that your breathing slows, and it becomes difficult to hold a stressful thought.

Once you are familiar with the technique you don't need to wiggle your fingers or use your hands to switch to peripheral vision. The more you practice the technique, the quicker you'll be able to switch between the two. It's an effective way to counter any stressful situation. Not just the stresses associated with public speaking.

CONFIDENCE ON DEMAND – ANCHORS

If you fear or are anxious about speaking in public, imagine if you could change those feelings to something more helpful, such as calm, confidence or excitement even, at the flick of a switch. An anchor is a technique that allows us to do just that. It creates an association between a stimulus and an emotion. We can choose an emotion we want to feel and associate it to a physical, audio, or visual trigger. For example, you could associate feeling confident with a physical trigger such as squeezing your thumb. Then, should you begin to feel anxious about an upcoming speaking engagement, simply squeeze your thumb to feel more confident.

As you read this you may be feeling a little sceptical but the great thing about this technique is, you are already using it. Is there a song, that when you hear it, you are taken back to a certain time of your life? It instantly puts a smile on your face and for a moment you re-experience how you felt back then. It could be the first dance song at your wedding or a song you remember being played when you were out with friends. You have created an auditory association or anchor between the song and how you felt at the time.

Anchors are a simple and effective technique commonly used by professional athletes, public speakers, and leaders of industry to maintain helpful emotional states such as confidence, motivation, energy and calm to name just a few. The next section provides step-by-step instructions so you can also learn how to use this technique.

How To Create An Anchor

1. Choose The Emotion You'd Like To Anchor

Decide what emotion would be helpful to you, calm, confident, motivated, energised. It's possible to create an anchor to any emotion so long as you've experienced that emotion in order to recreate it.

2. Identify A Trigger

Choose the trigger carefully. It must be accessible. Creating an anchor to your little toe could limit its use. Common anchor points are squeezing or rubbing knuckles and fingers. Some people hold or rub items of jewellery such as rings and necklaces. These work well so long as you don't tend to play with them. Imagine an anchor as a jug of water. It contains a certain amount of that emotion. The more water is poured from the jug, the less there is available and eventually, it will be empty. The more you use an anchor the more you deplete it. If you are accidentally triggering it, it may not be effective when you need it. Ensure the trigger is unique so it will only be triggered when you want to use it.

The trigger doesn't have to be physical. I know a speaker who anchored confidence to a particular song which she plays just before going on stage. But I recommend physical triggers whilst getting used to the technique as they are simple to use.

3. Associate The Emotion To The Trigger

Think of a time you experienced the emotion you want to anchor. The stronger the intensity of the memory the stronger the anchor will be. If you are anchoring 'relaxed', think of the most relaxed you've ever been. Think of that memory now, really immerse yourself into it. Notice what's around you, the sights, the sounds, how it feels, whether it's warm or cold. It takes a few seconds for the emotion associated with the memory to build and peaks between 5 to 15 seconds, before diminishing. It's the peak intensity that you want to associate with the anchor. Once you feel the strength of the memory peaking, trigger the anchor, and release it as soon as the strength of the emotion begins to wane.

If you struggle to recall a time when you felt a particular emotion intensely, you can instead imagine a time instead. The effect will be the same as the subconscious can't distinguish between real memories and imagination. For calm and relaxed, you could imagine laying on a tropical beach, on a perfect sunny day, or for excited and motivated you could imagine scoring the winning goal in a cup final.

4. Repeat The Association

The more times you repeat the process, the stronger the anchor. The rule of thumb is at least three to five times. You can use the same memory each time or different ones so long as the memories are intense. Remember to immerse yourself into the memory. Notice what's around you, see what you saw, hear what you heard and feel what you felt. The more detail you can recall the stronger the anchor will become.

5. Test The Anchor

Imagine a time in the future when you could do with more of the emotion you've anchored. Picture that time in your mind. Then trigger your anchor and notice the difference it makes. If you don't experience the emotion you've anchored, then repeat the process a few more times and test again. Once your anchor is formed you can use it to change your emotional state whenever you need to.

6. Keep The Anchor Topped Up

As mentioned previously, an anchor is like a jug of water. The more water we pour from the jug the less is available. The more we use an anchor the less effective it will be unless we top it up. Over time the strength of an anchor can also diminish. We can top up an anchor in the same way we created it. Recalling a time we felt the emotion intensely and triggering it. Another effective way to strengthen an anchor is to trigger it in any situation where we feel the emotion intensely. If you have created a calming anchor and you notice that you feel incredibly calm. Maybe when you are on holiday or just relaxing in the garden on a lazy Sunday afternoon. Trigger your anchor to top it up.

GAIN FRESH PERSPECTIVE

This is a really useful technique for anyone stressing about an upcoming event as it changes our perception of the event and shifts our focus from what may go wrong, to making sure it goes right. It is also referred to as the anxiety model. All that is required to successfully implement this technique is a little imagination.

Imagine you have your own personal time machine. Climb into it and float up into the air. See in the distance the upcoming event that you'd like to feel differently about.

1. Float forward in time to 15 minutes after the **successful** completion of the event and associate into your body (see the world through your eyes).

2. Notice how you feel differently now. Notice the reactions of those around you. Notice all the things that went well and how great you feel.

3. Climb back into your time machine, bringing all the learnings you've gained with you and return to the present time.

4. Now look at the upcoming event again and notice how your perception has changed.

This technique changes our subconscious perception of what will happen. Our anxiety is triggered by the assumption the event will go badly. Usually, when we consider this objectively we know this isn't true. Even the worst-case scenario isn't as bad as our anxiety is making us believe. By going forward in time, to 15 minutes after the successful completion of the event we remove the anxiety. It is impossible to feel anxious about something that has happened. We can feel regret, even remorse but we can't feel anxious. We can only feel anxious about things in the future.

By focussing on the 'successful completion' we change our assumption from a negative to a positive outcome. This allows us to view the event from a new perspective. As a result, we notice things we hadn't before, which affirms the assumption. When we then return to viewing the event in the future, our perspective has changed.

If you find your anxiety for an upcoming event impacts your ability to prepare or plan, you can add a step to the process above, immediately after step 3, 15 minutes after the successful completion of the event. Look back down the timeline to where you first entered the capsule. Notice all the actions you completed along the way to ensure success. Do this in reverse chronological order, noticing each as you look back down the timeline. This allows you to plan the activities without anxiety, as you are doing it from a position after the event has occurred.

How To Exit A Conversation Gracefully

A common fear for many is how to extract oneself from a conversation without offending or it becoming awkward. Pretty much in every social context, it is accepted, if not expected that at some point the conversation will come to an end. There are a couple of techniques that allow us to exit a conversation gracefully whilst maintaining the rapport and trust we've created.

Be Prepared

Have a few stock phrases or genuine explanations as to why you need to move on. Such as "It's been great catching up. I loved hearing about .... I need to catch up with a few people before they leave but hopefully, we'll get a chance to speak again later." Delivering such statements confidently ensures we maintain rapport.

Use Your Body Language

Turning our feet away from the person we are talking to and pointing them in the direction we'd prefer to go, sends a subconscious signal to the other party that it's time for the conversation to end. When we do this the other party is likely to pause and wait for us to announce our departure. Even if they do not pause, they are subconsciously prepared for us to deliver our exit statement. When using this technique, keep facing the other party but allow your torso to turn away.

4

HOW TO READ OTHERS

"Your body communicates as well as your mouth. Don't contradict yourself."

Allen Ruddock

When we think of great orators we tend to think of those who can energise and inspire with their words. Yet the core foundation of great communication is the ability to read and understand those we communicate with. By understanding our audience, we can choose the correct words and the delivery, so they have the biggest impact.

We are constantly sharing a wealth of information about ourselves through our physiology, facial expressions, and eye movements. This chapter examines what we can learn from facial expression and eye patterns and provides guidance on how to improve our ability to read others.

What is Non-Verbal Communication?

"Your body language, your eyes, your energy will come through to your audience before you even start speaking."

Peter Guber

Have you ever met a friend and asked how they are, but when they answer "well!" or "fine", you've instinctively known they are putting on a brave face? And when you have dug a little deeper your instincts were proven correct, and your friend was not in the good place they claimed. This is because you had accurately read their non-verbal communication, which was not congruent with what they were verbally saying.

We all instinctively read the body language of others whilst interpreting what they say. We use non-verbal communication in conjunction with the spoken word to emphasise our points of view and express our feelings.

You may have heard it said that the spoken word only accounts for 7% of human communication and that voice tone and physiology account for the remaining 93%. These numbers came from two studies undertaken by Professor Albert Mehrabian in the 1960s.

7%	Words
38%	Tonality
55%	Physiology

Figure 4.0

His studies have been widely misinterpreted and hotly contested within the scientific community. The percentages are often quoted as applying to all communication. If this was true, we should be able to understand 93% of any conversation regardless of the language spoken, just from voice tone and body language.

Mehrabian's research focussed on emotional incongruence, when what we say and how we say it differs from how we feel. It is in these scenarios where he found that we place greater emphasis on voice tone and physiology than the spoken word.

Whilst there is debate over the percentages, there is general agreement that people are more likely to believe our physiology and tone, over our words. Most of us prefer face-to-face communication. When we only have audio or a small image on a smartphone it is harder for us to correctly read the message we are receiving. By consciously understanding how non-verbal communication works, we can adapt our own communication style to gain the greatest impact. The first step to becoming a great non-verbal communicator is listening.

THE IMPORTANCE OF ACTIVE LISTENING

"The biggest communication problem is we do not listen to understand. We listen to reply"

Stephen Covey

When talking with others how often do you find yourself waiting for a gap in the dialogue so you can speak? It is a trap many of us fall into, being more focused on ourselves, what we are thinking or plan to say rather than paying attention to the other person's point of view.

When we are not fully engaged in a conversation there are consequences:

- The other party is usually aware. Either consciously or subconsciously. This can break rapport. As a result, when we speak, our words have less impact. How do you feel when it is obvious that the person you are talking to is not focused on what you are saying?

- We miss important verbal and non-verbal clues. When our attention is focused on our own thoughts, we can miss a huge amount of information both in terms of body language and tonality.

Covey's Levels Of Listening

How we listen can be categorised as follows.

- **Ignoring** – This is the lowest level of listening. Being physically present but totally disengaged.

- **Pretend** – Giving a pretence of listening. Saying things like 'I see' and 'OK' but not being fully aware of what has been said.

- **Selective** – This is when we pay attention to the speaker if they are talking about things we like or agree with.

- **Attentive** – This is when we are focused on the message from our particular point of view. How does what is being said impact us. What would we do in that situation? When attentively listening we can disengage to process what's been said and whether we agree or disagree.

- **Empathetic** – This is when we focus on what is being said and try to understand what is happening for the other party. When we are listening empathetically, we are alert to both verbal and non-verbal communication.

At the highest level of listening, empathetically, we receive a far more accurate impression of what is being communicated to us.

How To Develop Your Listening Skills

Many of us have formed bad listening habits. We have grown accustomed to spending most of our time at the lower end of Covey's scale. 'Ignoring', 'Pretending' and 'Selectively' listening to those around us. If we wish to improve our listening skills and notice more of the non-verbal clues people give us, practice is key.

Exercise

When next in a meeting or catching up with friends, see how long you can go without speaking. Use facial expressions and head movements to acknowledge what is being said. If you must, use phrases such as 'yes', 'I see', 'I understand' or even just sounds like 'mmm' or 'ah'.

At first, you may well struggle to do this for more than a minute or two but over time you will become more comfortable listening and observing. You may be amazed just how much the other person opens up and how much you discover about them

Open Questioning

"I have six serving men and true; they taught me all I know. Their names are what and where and when and how and why and who"

Rudyard Kipling

Asking questions demonstrates interest and encourages the other person to open up and talk. The type of questions we ask determines the quality of the responses we receive. Closed questions are those that only permit short, simple answers such as yes, or no. Whilst open questions allow the other party to control the direction of the conversation and share what's really important to them.

Open questions begin with: What, where, when, how, why, who and which. What happened next? When or how did you do that? Why is that important to you? Who was there? Which do you prefer and why?

Another great open question is, 'Tell me more about.....'

READING FACIAL EXPRESSIONS

"The most important thing in communication is to hear what isn't being said."

Peter Drucker

What To Look For

Our facial expressions provide a huge source of information. on how we think and feel. When we are angry our faces may flush noticeably. Anger triggers the body's fight or flight response increasing our heart rate and blood pressure. In turn, this raises the volume of blood in the capillaries close to the surface of the skin. As a result, our skin reddens. Swelling capillaries can also result in a noticeable change in the size of our lower lip.

We continually relax and tense our facial muscles. Some of these muscle changes are clearly visible. You may have noticed how some people tense their jaw when stressed or anxious? Other muscle changes are more subtle and go unnoticed unless we are specifically looking for them. These micro muscle changes affect how light is reflected from the skin, coursing skin tone to change.

The way we breathe alters depending upon our environment and how we feel. It can be fast or slow, long, or short, physically low down from the stomach or high up in the chest. When we are anxious, our breathing tends to be high in the chest, fast and shallow. Whilst relaxed it tends to be low down, slow and long.

Eye movements also provide a wealth of information. The next time you engage someone in conversation, notice how their eyes move around whilst talking. Depending on what we are experiencing our pupils may dilate or contract. The speed and frequency of our blinking also vary. I have previously mentioned when we experience strong emotions, most of us look down and to the right. Hence the phrase 'downright angry'. Whilst when we recall a picture in our mind, we look up. We will cover how to read eye movement later.

Our facial expressions are unique to us. It can be misleading and dangerous to draw universal conclusions, such as certain facial expressions indicating lying or telling the truth. But there are patterns in our expressions. We demonstrate the same or similar characteristics each time we experience the same or similar emotion. Once we understand or have calibrated these patterns, we can gain an insight into what someone else is experiencing simply by observing their facial expressions and physiology.

The BLESS mnemonic, figure 4.1, provides a convenient way to remember the key elements to observe whilst reading someone's non-verbal communication.

B	Breathing	Rate/Location
L	Lower lip size	Lines/No lines
E	Eyes	Focused/Unfocused Constricted/Dilated pupils
S	Skin tone	Shiny/Dull
S	Skin colour	Dark/Light

Figure 4.1

Calibration

Calibration involves observing someone and noticing how their behaviours deviate from the norm. For example, if a person is sitting with their legs stretched out in front of them, and suddenly withdraws their feet under the chair, that is a deviation from baseline behaviour. We all instinctively calibrate other people. If you consider the people you know best, family members, close friends; I am sure you would be able to tell, just by looking at them, whether they were happy, sad, frustrated, or relaxed. We are all naturally good at this. By becoming consciously aware of the baseline behaviours of others, we can further improve our ability to read them.

Exercise – Improve Your Ability To Read Others

- *Find a willing partner (you can run this exercise on your own by recording yourself and then watching the footage).*

- *Ask your partner to think of someone they really like. As they think of that person calibrate their facial expressions. Notice the changes.*

- *Next, ask them to think of someone they strongly dislike and again note their facial expressions.*

If your partner is struggling to think of someone they dislike, they can think of food instead.

- *Repeat this calibration process a few times.*

- *Then ask your partner to randomly think of someone (or food) they either like or dislike and see if you can tell which it is by reading their facial expressions.*

The more you practice reading and calibrating facial expressions, the more easily it will come to you.

Practical Example

When I work with corporate teams, I calibrate individual team members. I am particularly interested in their facial characteristics and physiology when they agree and disagree. It can be difficult in a work setting, surrounded by peers, to say what we genuinely think. So, when I propose a course of action and everyone verbally agrees, yet not everyone's expressions are congruent with what they have said, I get an early indication of who I need to spend more time with.

I also keenly observe when leaders provide team updates. Through people's reactions, I can usually determine who is on board and where further conversations are required.

I also find calibration incredibly valuable with family members. A few years ago, my eldest son came home from school and proceeded to argue and fight with everyone. He was seven at the time, so the occasional outburst was to be expected. But this was different. His behaviour and facial expressions did not match his typical naughty behaviour. I calmed him down and used the 'Clean Language' patterns, covered later in this book, to help uncover what was really going on. My son is of mixed African and European heritage. That day he had experienced racial bullying for the first time and was struggling to process it. By being able to read his body language and being curious about what I was seeing, I was able to help him come to terms with it and work with his school to ensure it stopped.

Just imagine all the places in your life where this technique could help you. As with all the techniques in this book, the key to success is practice, practice, practice.

INTERPRETING EYE MOVEMENT

"Pretend not, for I can read your eyes"

Sheetal Desai

How Our Eyes Move Whilst We Think

Our eye movement provides an insight into our internal thought process. Imagine the brain is a large filing cabinet. When we access visual information, our eyes look up as we process it. When we access auditor information (remember or imagine sounds) our eyes move horizontally and when we process kinaesthetic information (recalling or imagining physical activity or emotions) or auditory digital information (processing or analysing our thoughts or data) our eyes look down.

We all fall into one of two categories. Approximately 80% of people are **Normally Organised**, as illustrated in Figure 4.2. When a normally organised person pictures a memory in their mind, such as their first day at school, they will look up and to the right (our right, their left). When they imagine or construct an image such as the perfect, golden beach, they will look up and to the left.

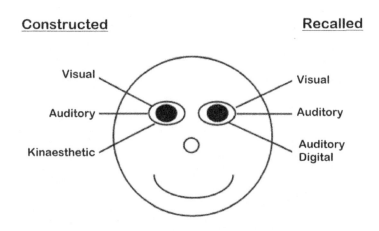

Figure 4.2 Normally Organised. The image as you look at a person.

Whilst recalling their favourite song, they will look horizontally right. Whilst imagining or constructing a sound such as their favourite song played backwards or a world leader talking after inhaling helium, they look horizontally left.

When analysing information or listening to critical self-talk (processing **Auditory Digital** information) they look down and to the right. Whilst experiencing emotions or considering physical activity (processing **Kineathetic** information) they look down and to the left.

The remaining 20% of the population are referred to as reverse organised, as illustrated in figure 4.3. This is the mirror opposite of normally organised.

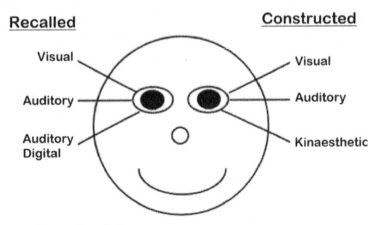

Figure 4.3 Reverse Organised

Determine Normally or Reverse Organised

To interpret the meaning of eye movements, we must first determine whether someone is 'Normally' or 'Reverse'

organised. This can be done very easily by asking questions
that have specific types of answers.

Exercise

- *Find a willing partner and using the 'Eye Movement
  Questions' determine whether they are 'Normally' or
  'Reverse' organised. Compare their eye movements to
  the illustrations in figures 4.2 and 4.3.*

- *Whilst talking with your partner note if their eyes tend
  to migrate to one particular representational system.
  I.E. Do they tend to look up, across or down when they
  talk?*

Eye Movement Questions

The following questions will direct a recipient's eyes to the
stated representational system.

Visual Remembered	What colour was the room you grew up in?
	Can you picture the colour of your first bike/car?
	What did your favourite toy/friend look like when you were a young child?
Visual Constructed	What would your room/car look like if it were blue?
	What would your house look like overgrown with ivy?
	What would I look like with spiky hair?

What would it look like if a zebra had a giraffe's head and a kangaroo's tail?

Auditory Remembered	What was the very last thing I said?
	Can you sing your favourite song to yourself?
	Remember the sound of your mother's/boss'/partner's voice?
	What did your favourite song in school sound like?
Auditory Constructed	What would I sound like if I had Donald Duck's voice/inhaled helium?
	What would it sound like in an echo chamber?
	What would your car horn be like if it sounded like a foghorn?
Kinaesthetic (feelings, sense of touch, taste, smell)	What does it feel like to put on wet socks?
	What does it feel like to hold a baby?
	Remember the feeling of walking along the beach barefoot?
	What does your favourite food taste like?
Auditory Digital (internal dialogue)	Recite a prayer or poem to yourself?
	What do you say to yourself when things go wrong/right?
	Can you say your three times table to yourself in your head?

What We Can Learn From Eye Movement

By reading and understanding eye movement we can tailor our communication to best suit our audience.

Preferred Communication Styles

Imagine you have a meeting with an important client or have an interview for a job you really want. You have a short window to make a great impression. Understanding eye movements provides an opportunity to do just that. Each of us has a preferred communication style. When we receive information in that style we are more likely to pay attention to it. By altering our communication style so it reflects the preferred style of our audience we increase the likelihood of our message landing well.

We can determine the preferred communication style of others by observing their eye movements. If a person spends most of their time, during a conversation looking up, they are likely to have a strong preference for visual information. If they spend most of the time looking along the horizon plane, they are likely to have a preference for auditory information. If they look down a lot, they either prefer kinaesthetic language or are auditory digital (analytical thinking).

For those with a visual preference, a slide deck presentation may land perfectly. Whilst a person with an auditory preference needs to hear your message. They want the scene described to them. Those with a kinaesthetic preference may prefer you to sketch out your ideas on a whiteboard and walk them through it. Whilst those with an analytical preference need to know the facts and data behind your ideas and conclusions.

Having the ability to quickly determine someone else's communication preferences and change our style accordingly is incredibly powerful for winning someone over to our point of view. I once presented to the CTO of a large wealth management company, my ideas on how he could improve productivity. I had prepared an artistic 11-slide presentation. It was our first meeting, and I was unaware he had a strong auditory communication preference. We did not get past the first slide. He could not concentrate on the visual material. He wanted to ask questions and discuss my findings. After that meeting, I adapted my communication style. I kept the visuals to a minimum and engaged in discussion.

Physiological Clues To Communication Preferences

Eye movement is not the only way to determine the representation system or communication preference of a person. There are other physical characteristics.

Communication Preference	Common Physiological Characteristics
Visual	<ul><li>Look up when thinking and talking</li><li>Keep their bodies upright whether seated or standing</li><li>Fairly rapid breathing from high up in the chest</li><li>Organised</li><li>Talk quickly</li><li>Observant</li><li>Can struggle to remember verbal instructions</li></ul>

	• Good spellers
	• Use visual descriptions when communicating
	• Visual learning preference(must see things to understand them
Auditory	• Eyes mostly remain on the horizontal plane (move sideways) when thinking and talking
	• Breathe from the middle of their chest
	• Easily distracted by noise and external sounds
	• Can repeat things back easily
	• Learn by listening
	• Speak rhythmically
	• Moves lips/speak words whilst reading
	• Talk to themselves
	• Tend to use auditory descriptions when communicating
	• Memorise procedures sequentially
	• Like to hear feedback
Kinaesthetic	• Look down when thinking and talking

	- Slow, deep breathing from the bottom of the lungs - Talk and move slowly - Pace whilst thinking and gesture whilst talking - Tend to be physical (touchy-feely) - Can stand quite close to people - Use kinaesthetic descriptions when communicating - Learn through doing - They need to know if the information/communication "feels" right
Auditory Digital	- Internally analyse their thoughts and opinions - Logical and analytical in their approach - Can be dissociated from feelings and emotions - Use logical and analytical phrases when communicating - Learn through 'making sense of things' - Can take on the characteristics of other representational systems

Ways To Build Trust & Rapport

You may recall from chapter two, we naturally warm to those who look, behave and sound like us. The language we use provides an insight into who we are and how we think. By matching the language we use to that of our audience, we can quickly create a strong connection or rapport, ensuring our message is more likely to be heard by them.

Those with a visual communication preference tend to use visual language. They may describe how they 'see' a situation, whilst an auditory person uses auditory language. They may describe how the situation 'sounds'. A kinaesthetic person may describe how they 'feel' about a situation, whilst an auditory digital person will say what they 'think' about it. The same is true for phrases and metaphors.

The following tables illustrate the words and phrases commonly used by people according to their language or representational system preference. Having a preference for one does not prevent us from using the words and phrases associated with the others. We just tend to use those associated with our preference more frequently.

Predicate Words:

Visual	Auditory	Kinaesthetic	Auditory Digital
See	Hear	Feel	Sense
Look	Listen	Touch	Experience
View	Sound	Grasp	Understand
Appear	Announce	Get hold of	Think/thought
Show	Harmonise	Slip through	Learn

Fade	Tune in	Catch on	Process
Reveal	Tune out	Tap into	Decide
Envision	All ears	Make contact	Motivate
Illuminate	Silence	Throw out	Consider
Imagine	Be heard	Turn around	Change
Clear	Resonate	Hard	Perceive
Flash	Quiet	Unfeeling	Insensitive
Focused	Melodious	Concrete	Distinct
Hazy	Dissonance	Scrape	Conceive
Crystal	Question	Get a handle	Know
Picture	Unhearing	Solid	Describe
Dawn	View/review	Impression	Be conscious
Foggy	Deaf	Sensation	Analise
Vivid	Attune	Expand	Decipher
Inspect	Shout	Shiver	Conscious
Notice	Ring	Rush	Recall
Dim	Cry	Move	Communicate
Watch	Articulate	Warm	
Outlook	Mention	Flow	
Glance	Whine	Hold	

The following are examples of everyday phrases.

Visual	Auditory
I see what you're saying	That sounds great
I get the picture	It has clarity
Looks like/good	It rings a bell
I like the look of this	It fell on deaf ears
I've had an eye full	I hear/like what you're saying
It appears to me	Blabbermouth
A shadow of a doubt	Clear as a bell
Bird's eye view	Clearly expressed
What's on the horizon	Call on
Catch a glimpse of	Describe in detail
Clear cut	Earful
Clear as ... day	Give an account of
Dim view	Give me your ear
Flashed on/up	Grant an audience
Get a perspective on	Hold your tongue
Get a scope on	Idle talk
Hazy idea	Inquire into
In light of	Keynote speaker
Looks like	Loud and clear

Make a scene	Manner of speaking
Mental image	Say no more
Let's look at this later	Let's discuss/speak later

Kinaesthetic	Auditory Digital
That feels right	Afterthought
I get a gut feeling	Hold that thought
I get a sense of that	This makes sense
I'm in touch with that idea	To make sense of
I'll pick that up with you later	It's logical
The penny dropped	There's no logic in that
Hold fire	The specifications are correct
All washed up	I would appreciate your thoughts
Boils down to	I'll consider the idea
Chip off the old block	I'll take it under advisement
Come to grips with	To sum up
Control yourself	Have you done the due diligence?
Cool/calm/collected	I Remember discussing that
Firm foundations	Let's consider this later
Get a handle on	That goes against all the evidence
Get a load of this	
Get in touch with	

Get the drift of	Let's consider the facts
Hand in hand	Why take the risk
Hang in there	
Heated argument	
Hold it/on	
Hothead	

An Insight Into Learning Preferences

How we subconsciously filter sensory information influences our learning preferences. By understanding our communication preferences and those of others we can choose the most effective learning medium. Those with a kinaesthetic preference may struggle with traditional, classroom-based learning, preferring activity-based learning. Movement and learning by doing are important to them. Those with a visual preference tend to learn best using charts, illustrations, and colour. Those with an analytical preference need to understand why, they want the value and reason behind the learning. Whilst those with an auditory preference fare well in lecture rooms and listening to podcasts.

Reading Emotions

We can gain insight into someone's emotional state by observing their eye movements. If someone is spending a lot of time looking down and to their right (or left if reverse organised) they are likely to be processing emotions. A simple way to aid someone upset or anxious is to encourage them to look up. It activates the visual regions of the brain and can take the edge off the emotion.

Determining Truthfulness

You may have heard it is possible to tell when someone is lying by their eye movement. Specifically, they look to the left when lying. This stems from the fact most people look up to their left when they construct an image. For example, if we asked someone who is normally organised, what they did last night, their eyes will move up and to their left as they recall the memory. Should their eyes instead move up and to their right, they may be constructing a new, alternative version of events, or fabricating a lie.

Eye movement on its own is highly inaccurate in determining if someone is lying. First, we must correctly assess whether the person is 'Normally' or 'Reverse Organised'. Then there are numerous reasons why someone may look up and to the left, other than lying. These are explained in the section 'Challenges Interpreting Eye Movements'. Drawing conclusions from eye patterns alone can be misleading and dangerous. But they do provide a good insight into what may be going on and when further questioning may be beneficial.

Challenges When Interpreting Eye Movement

When interpreting eye patterns, here are a few points to be aware of:

- Eye movements are not always clean. For example, if I asked someone to imagine their front door painted blue with pink dots, they may first need to remember their front door before constructing a new image in their mind. So, their eyes will first move one way, then the other.

- When asked a question we may initially imagine the answer the questioner desires before giving the truthful answer, or a stray thought may pop into our head. This could cause our eyes to briefly move to construct. This could be misinterpreted as making up an alternative answer.

- Occasionally, when we ask someone a question, their eyes may dart around. This is referred to as a **trans-derivational search**. It occurs because our minds are initially unsure how to process the question.

DETERMINE YOUR OWN COMMUNICATION PREFERENCE

If you would like to know your personal communication preferences complete the short questionnaire in Appendix I.

5

HARNESS THE POWER OF LANGUAGE

"The way we talk to our children becomes their inner voice"

Peggy O'Mara

Language is an essential part of human communication. Words give meaning to our thoughts and experiences. We use language to understand and be understood. Yet language is much more than the logical exchange of data. Our choice of language provides insight into who we are, our values and our beliefs. By paying close attention to people's language, we can learn so much about them. When combined with an understanding of the subconscious impact of language, we can inspire, motivate and influence others.

This chapter covers the language patterns used by coaches and therapists to bring about change in their clients and by scriptwriters, salespeople, and politicians to inspire, energise and influence their audience.

PLANTING IDEAS - LINGUISTIC PRESUPPOSITIONS

When we communicate our words express our thoughts and experiences. Our audience hears the words and processes them, creating a mental picture of what we have described. However, the picture our audience creates is bound to be different from our own.

Consider the following statement, "In the park this morning I saw a dog chase a ball," It is unlikely you have created the same mental image as I had, when I wrote the statement. You may picture a small terrier whilst I, a Great Dane. Your dog may be white, whilst mine brown, or black? Yours chasing a tennis ball whilst mine a football? How have you imagined the park? Are there trees, shrubs and flowers or swings and roundabouts?

The different permutations are endless. Yet these differences do not stop the flow of conversation, they enable it. If we had to describe every scene in minute detail for dialogue to work it would be overly long and drawn-out. Instead, we subconsciously make assumptions about the information we share, in the belief our audience will be able to deconstruct our words and create an internal representation or mental image, which is similar enough for the dialogue to make sense. These assumptions are referred to as presuppositions.

Why Presuppositions Are So Powerful

Because we must mentally process a statement to understand it, we must also mentally process any presuppositions it contains. The presuppositions we use in our language can have a big impact on those around us whether intentional or not.

As a child, were you told to "be careful" or "stay safe" as you left the house? It is common parental advice that can be counterproductive. It presupposes there is external danger without providing any specifics. To process the statement a child must subconsciously accept the assumption. Studies suggest that children who are frequently told to take care or be careful as they leave home tend to be more anxious than those who are given positive instructions such as *'have a great day.' 'enjoy yourself,* or *'have fun.'*

When my children were young, I would pick them up from primary school. When I walked through the playground it was common to hear the tears of children who'd fallen and scrapped an elbow or knee. Often, I also heard a parent telling a tearful son to; "Stop crying, don't be a girl." Or words to that effect. I wonder what impact such words have on the next generation of young men. The statement presupposes expressing hurt is a weakness, connected to masculinity. It also implies being 'a girl' is an insult. Bearing in mind how men can struggle to talk about emotional issues and the continued glass ceiling many women experience in the workplace, I can not help but feel these parents were unintentionally perpetuating both.

Well-crafted sentences using positively intentioned presuppositions can generate great results. All parents know how difficult it can be to get information from their children about their school day. "How was your day?", is usually rewarded with a one-word answer, "fine" or "OK". Whilst the right presuppositions can trigger their thought processes.

Consider this alternative question, 'What was the best thing you learnt today?' This presupposes there were multiple learnings of differing value. When I use this type of question with my children, they immediately start reflecting on the day's events. Once these thought processes are activated they are far more likely to share what is on their mind. Similar questions I ask are: 'who's had the best day?', 'what was the funniest thing that happened?' and 'what were you most happy about?'.

Presuppositions are also effective at changing negative thinking. I frequently work with people who have an aversion to public speaking. As an event draws near, they can focus on the worst-case scenario. What if they forget their lines or freeze? I challenge these unhelpful thought processes with statements such as 'Just imagine how great it will feel when you have successfully completed it.' This presupposes the event will be a success and they will feel great. They must imagine this scenario, even if briefly, to process the statement. This moves them away from a negative, anxious state of mind to a more positive one.

By deciding which assumptions or presuppositions we want others to focus on and embedding them into our dialogue, we can directly influence their thought processes. It doesn't necessarily mean that the seeds we plant will grow. People have free will and may reject the presuppositions. But they must at first consider them before they can reject them. Often that's all it takes.

The Key To Using Linguistic Presuppositions

To effectively use Linguistic Presuppositions we must;

- Be self-aware. Think about what you say before you say it
- Avoid inadvertently embedding negative or unhelpful assumptions into sentences
- Construct sentences containing the positive assumptions that could benefit those we are communicating with.

Examples

Linguistic Presuppositions that can have a negative impact;

- What's wrong?
- Take care/be safe!
- What if you are wrong/loose?
- What's the worst that can happen?
- Don't be afraid!
- Don't be stupid

Linguistic Presuppositions that can have a positive impact;

- Have a great day!
- Be yourself, you are great!
- Whatever happens, you've got this!
- You can do this!
- Be courageous, take a risk!
- Focus on your work!
- Worst case, you'll be just fine!

Linguistic presuppositions also provide the basis of the next two language patterns in this chapter, conversational hypnosis and meta-language.

Conversational Hypnosis (Language of Influence)

How often, whether in the workplace or a social setting, do you find yourself wishing you could inspire, motive or challenge those around you? Yet either you lack the words or your words are met with irremovable resistance.

Hypnotic language provides us with a set of simple phrases, that when used correctly, allow us to communicate with others on a deeper level and achieve great results.

During this section, we will cover, what hypnosis and hypnotic language are, how they work and how we can use them to inspire, motivate and challenge others. By the end of it, you will be familiar with simple hypnotic language and be able to use it to positive effect with friends, family and colleagues.

Before proceeding let me address the concerns some have about hypnosis. The techniques described in this section will not enable you to practice mind control. You will not be able to use them on others, so they do things against their will. If that is your aim, then this is the wrong book for you.

What Is Hypnosis?

You are probably familiar with the term 'trance'. It is often associated with hypnosis. The word may conjure images of people in a deep sleep or a stage hypnosis show. A trance state occurs when the conscious mind takes a back seat, and our subconscious thinking comes to the foreground. Have you ever taken a walk or gone for a drive and switched off as you travel along? You arrive at your destination and realise you have been on autopilot. You were in a state of trance. You were so familiar with what you were doing that you consciously switched off and allowed your subconscious or auto-pilot to take over. Had anything out of the ordinary occurred during that journey, such as a car pulling in front of you, your conscious thinking would have taken over so you could act appropriately.

We naturally go into trance all the time. If we didn't, we'd find it impossible to sleep, as trance is part of the natural sleep cycle. We tend to be in a trance state when we are absorbed by something or are concentrating very hard. Our conscious thinking processes turn down whilst we are in deep thought. By using hypnotic language, we can bring about a momentary trance in others, bypassing their conscious filters and therefore communicating with them on a much deeper level.

Why is this important? Think of a time you were complimented; the chances are you consciously rejected the compliment. You may have downplayed the achievement, or accredited others. Or maybe you questioned the motives of those who complimented you. How about the last time you were insulted or criticised? Did you consciously reject that or take it to heart?

We have evolved to be consciously critical of ourselves. It is a strategy that has served us as a species. It has driven us to be better and to stay alive. On occasion, it can be self-defeating. I am sure we can all think of times when our self-criticism has hindered rather than helped us.

This filtering process can also mean at times, that others don't fully consider our opinions and ideas. Our suggestions can be dismissed without receiving the proper consideration they deserve. Or what we say may be distorted or rejected due to the predetermined views of others. During this section we will cover simple hypnotic language that enables us to bypass the stubborn, mental programming of others, ensuring our words are heard and truly considered.

What Is Hypnotic Language?

Hypnotic language provides a simple and effective way to inspire and influence others. As with presuppositions, it allows the recipient to create their own, personalised meaning. It is also referred to as Milton language after Milton H. Erickson, who was widely acknowledged as the world's foremost practitioner and teacher of hypnosis. As a therapist, he used a combination of artfully vague language and trance to bring about real, lasting change in his clients.

You are already familiar with many of these language patterns as they are used extensively by politicians and marketeers to convey a personalised, often emotive message to influence their audience.

Getting Started

Hypnotic language can be incredibly simple. Whenever we use words that evoke the imagination, such as 'imagine', 'picture' or 'recall', we are encouraging those listening to focus internally or go into a trance-like state.

- Imagine just how good it will be when you have mastered these language patterns.

- Picture yourself as a highly effective communicator.

- Recall all the techniques you have learnt so far and imagine the results you can attain by using them.

Sport and Life Coaches frequently use these simple words when coaching clients as they can quickly bring about a shift

in the client's thinking. This is illustrated in the following
scenarios.

Scenario 1 – Goal setting

When we imagine or recall ourselves achieving a goal we
create an internal representation or image of that success. We
will picture in our mind what it looks like. This has a
neurological impact. Our emotional state will change to
reflect that of the event. For example, if we imagine or recall a
sad or happy event, we are likely to begin feeling sad or
happy.

When we picture ourselves attaining success, it can not only
change how we feel about the challenge, but it can also:

- Increase our confidence.
- Increase our motivation. As we now believe it's
  possible.
- Reduce any stress we may have been feeling.
- Increase our desire to achieve more.

We can test this by just picturing ourselves achieving a goal.
What is the thing you most want to accomplish over the next
year? Imagine yourself realising that goal. Create that image
in your mind, now. Notice where you are and what you are
doing. Notice how you feel as you picture success?

Do you feel differently about that goal now?

Scenario 2 – Changing Negative Emotions

Many of us, from time to time may experience unhelpful
emotions such as fear, worry and anxiety. By simply recalling

or imagining a situation where we naturally experience more helpful emotions, such as feeling calm and relaxed we can begin to change how we actually feel.

Again this is easy to test. Just imagine you are relaxing on the most perfect beach. The sand is brilliant white, whilst the sky is the most perfect blue. Hear the rolling waves in the distance gently crash against the shore. Feel the soothing warmth of the sun on your skin and the occasional, gentle breeze. Notice what's around you, all the noises, the smells, as you feel more and more relaxed.

The chances are, you are beginning to feel relaxed. This is a simple and effective technique that can be used with anyone. If you have a colleague or friend who is overly stressed, simply encouraging them to recall or imagine an event or activity they enjoy or find relaxing will change their emotional state. For example, where are you going on holiday? What are you doing at the weekend? Followed by questions that will encourage them to picture the experience such as; that sounds relaxing or exciting or what will you do? Or what's the best part of that?

Seven Simple Hypnotic Language Patterns

The following language patterns provide a good introduction to Hypnotic language. Don't worry about the category names. You don't need to know the categories to use the language effectively.

Lost Performative - Judgement without stating who is judging.

- Let us make our country great again. (Who says it isn't now? What one person perceives as great may differ from another's).

- The health system is at a tipping point. (According to who? Where is the evidence).

- It's never been so bad! (Says who?).

The above statements or variations of these are used frequently by politicians. They place a seed in people's minds yet provide no detail. For each statement, the person hearing it creates their own interpretation that is relevant and personal to them.

Universal Qualifier - These are generalisations that do not specify what or who we are referring to. They are recognised using the following words: 'all', 'every', 'never', 'always', 'nobody'

- We're all in this together.

- We all know ..... is the party of law and order.

- Every vote for me is a vote that counts.

As with the previous example, these statements are artfully vague and can be used to place a seed or idea in people's minds.

Cause And Effect - Implying one thing leads to another. When this is presupposed it tends to be accepted. These statements follow the format; If.... then..... or As you..... then you

- If you practice a language pattern every day, in no time at all, you will become proficient.

We are more likely to accept the connection between 'cause' and 'effect' in a statement if it follows a series of obviously true cause and effect statements. Political speechwriters frequently use this technique. Do the following sound familiar?

> *"Financial mismanagement has led to increasing levels of debt and higher taxes.*
>
> *The decisions they have made have impacted our economy, schools and health care system.*
>
> *A vote for us will bring about the change you want and deserve."*

Complex Equivalent - When one thing equals another.

- The more you study the more you will learn.
- A vote for me is a vote for change.

As with Cause and Effect, we are more likely to accept the connection between the Complex Equivalent in a statement if it follows a series of obviously true statements.

Embedded Commands - Instructions embedded in a sentence that directs someone to do something. Our conscious mind hears one message whilst the subconscious hears another.

- You, **like me**, are passionate about personal development.
- People who **trust me** are a good judge of character.

Like me/ Trust me are the embedded command. This technique is often used by salespeople as we are more likely to buy from those we trust and like, as well as politicians. Consciously we hear one message whilst subconsciously we hear the embedded command.

Tag Question - A question tagged to the end of a statement designed to remove resistance to the statement.

- We can all learn language patterns, **can't we**?
- You are starting to master these patterns now, **aren't you**?

You may find as you read the statements above that you nod your head in agreement. They subconsciously reinforce the message within the main statement.

Double Bind - Providing the illustration of free choice whilst leading the recipient along a predetermined path.

- Do you want to go to bed now or after a story?

The above statement I used a lot with my children when they were young. Nine times out of ten they choose after the story. Very rarely do they challenge and request an option not given. In contrast, when I said, "It's bedtime", I would receive a huge pushback. "It's not fair, why do my friends get to stay up later." By using a double bind, I created the parameters for the conversation. Their energy was focused on the outcome they most wanted, a book then bed. Whilst I was happy with either option.

- Will you send me the report today or tomorrow?

Using the above statement in a work context is likely to have a different outcome than asking 'By when will the report be ready.'

- Would you like Chinese or Italian for dinner?

If we are happy with both options, this question increases the likelihood of us having a meal we want whilst allowing the other person to feel they are in charge.

Layering Hypnotic Language

When we combine these simple hypnotic patterns, they become even more effective. Consider the following statements. Notice the language patterns within the text.

Example 1

It's been a challenging year, hasn't it? We've all had hard struggles to overcome. But there's light on the horizon and by working together we will create the brighter future we all want.

Everyone who reads the statement above will derive their own meaning. Let us deconstruct the statement.

It's been a challenging year.

This is a lost performative. It presupposes the recipient has had a challenging year. If I asked the question 'Have you had a challenging year?' some may say yes whilst others no. By presupposing it's been a challenging year, the recipient subconsciously accepts the assumption and begins searching for reasons why the year has been challenging. The word 'challenging' is vague. It means different things to different people and provides our imagination with a wide remit.

Hasn't it?

A tag question. It presupposes agreement and thus breaks down any internal resistance to the statement. Doesn't it?

We have all had hard struggles to overcome.

This statement contains both a universal qualifier and a lost performative. The presupposition that we have had struggles is a fair bet, but my struggles are likely to be very different to yours. By presupposing struggles, again the subconscious mind starts searching for them.

But there's light on the horizon

'But' is often referred to as a power word. It has a hidden subconscious interpretation. When we hear it, we tend to diminish the value of what came before and place greater emphasis on what follows. 'Light on the horizon' is a powerful metaphor. It tells a story all on its own. (See the section on metaphors for more information on why they are a powerful form of communication). What light? Which horizon? We create our own meaning for each.

By working together, we will create a brighter future we all want.

If this were a question, "Can we build a brighter future by working together?" it would have a very different impact. You may start to consider both sides of the argument. Presupposing that a brighter future is a certainty, so long as we work together, encourages us to believe it's true.

Example 2

Studying and practising hypnotic language patterns is the key to artfully using them. You will achieve what you want when you practice.

The statement contains two complex equivalents and an embedded command. The presuppositions lead you to the conclusion that 'study' and 'practice' are key, and what you want to achieve is possible.

In contrast consider the impact of the following statement: "You need to practice, or you will fail!" a very common statement when I was at school.

Example 3

To provide a little context, I heard the following example at an exhibition where a salesman was encouraging people to buy his product. After answering a lady's question, he added his own, shown below. At this point, the lady in question had not indicated whether she intended to buy the product or not.

'Would you like to pay by credit card or debit?"

This double-bind provides the illusion of choice whilst presupposing that the recipient will buy the product. Had the salesman asked, would you like to buy, subconsciously she would have begun considering her options. Instead, her thought processes were artfully focused on the best way to pay.

In case you are wondering, the lady in the example paid by credit card. Presuppositions are immensely powerful, as you will realise when you go out and use them. Won't you?

Example 4

Consider all you have learnt whilst reading this book. All the techniques and self-awareness that will help you become a more effective communicator. Because the more you practice these techniques the better you will become at using them. We all know that practice is the key to success, don't we? If you practice a little every day, in no time at all you will become truly proficient.

Imagine where and how you can use these techniques in the future. Picture yourself a year from now using them confidently. Note the impact you have on those around you and how great it feels to communicate the way you do. And all it took to achieve this was a little practice.

Key Points

- Hypnotic language is vague, allowing the recipient to place their own interpretations on our words.
- It allows us to communicate directly with the subconscious, bypassing the conscious filters.
- It evokes a trance state whereby those we speak to focus internally as opposed to externally.
- Rapport is key. 'Pace and Lead' until you have built rapport to achieve the best results.

Self-Coaching Exercise

This exercise uses hypnotic language patterns to challenge our perceptions or beliefs about ourselves. We all from time-to-time experience limiting or unhelpful thinking that hinders or prevents us from achieving what we want. For example, imposter syndrome, thinking we not good enough. Yet when we consider the facts, we know these thoughts aren't justified.

If you have a goal or challenge and your negative, critical thinking is holding you back, try the following:

1. Identify an area of your life where more self-confidence or belief would be beneficial.
2. Write the following statements on separate pieces of paper.
   o Just imagine you can do what you want to. Picture it now in your mind. Notice how good it feels achieving that goal.
   o You've achieved so much in life already, haven't you? Recall those challenges now and how you overcame them.
   o Just as you've succeeded before you will succeed with this, won't you?
   o You know you can do this, don't you?
3. Place the paper face down and mix them up.
4. Start by asking yourself the question, 'What do you want to have happen?' Once you've answered the question, in turn, pick up a piece of paper and ask yourself the question on it.
5. Continue until you have asked yourself all the questions.
6. Take a moment to notice how you feel now.

Taking Hypnotic Language To The Next Level

Once you are comfortable using the seven patterns covered so far you can add more to your repertoire. Appendix II contains an extensive list of hypnotic languages.

CHALLENGING STRONGLY HELD VIEWS - METALANGUAGE

How often do you encounter friends or colleagues whose ideas clash with yours? Or who hold beliefs about themselves and their ability which is evidently untrue and prevents them from achieving their aspirations? Often, we avoid challenging these ideas as it can lead to arguments and conflict.

In this section we will explore how Metalanguage can provide insights into another person's thought processes and enable us to effectively challenge their strongly held ideas, limiting beliefs or destructive habits.

What Is Meta-Language

Meta-language derives from the work undertaken by family therapists Virginia Satir and Fritz Pearls. They achieved remarkable success using very specific language, to encourage their clients to reflect on past events and draw new conclusions.

We have subconscious filters or thought processes that we use to make sense of the world around us. How we perceive any situation is based on multiple factors including our personal experiences, values and beliefs. See chapter 1, 'The Science of Communication', for a more detailed explanation. Sometimes we draw inaccurate unhelpful conclusions which become embedded into our subconscious thinking, negatively impacting the decisions we make.

The words we use to express our thoughts, ideas and feelings provide clues to our deeper thought processes. By paying attention to these clues and asking appropriate Meta-questions, we can challenge the conclusions that others have drawn.

For example, have you ever had the following or similar conversation?

Friend: *"Everyone at work hates me!"*.

You: *"Why do you say that?"*

Friend: *"I can tell by the way they look at me"*.

The friend in this situation has made a big generalisation based on very little information. They have created a belief concerning how their work colleagues feel about them. It is highly unlikely for their statement to be true, but tackling the belief head-on, 'of course they don't', 'you are being silly', or 'I don't believe that', is unlikely to change their negative view. It is more likely to terminate the conversation and possibly further embed the belief.

Meta-questions, direct people to reevaluate the situation and revisit their own assumptions and beliefs. Contrast the previous conversation to the following:

Friend: *"Everyone at work hates me.*

You: *What makes you say that?*

Friend: *I can tell by the way they all look at me.*

You: *What, everyone?*

Friend: *Well, most of them.*

You: *Who specifically?*

Friend: *Simon*

You: *So, it's just Simon?*

Friend: *Yes*

You: *And how do you know he hates you?*

Friend: *He never says, 'good morning'.*

You: *So, everyone who doesn't say good morning to you hates you?"*

In the second scenario, the friend re-evaluates the situation. On reflection, the entire world is not against them. Just one person. Even that is less certain now.

Meta-Questions – Getting Started

Using the following five Meta-questions we can achieve great results. Once you are comfortable with them you can add more from the full list.

Who	.....specifically?
What	.....specifically?
When	.....specifically?
Where	.....specifically?
How	.....specifically?

Take Care when asking 'Why?'. E.g. Why do you think that? It triggers the subconscious to search for evidence to back up the belief or view. It is likely to strengthen rather than challenge it.

Examples

Statement	Meta-Questions
I'll never be any good at	• When did you decide that? • What makes you say this? • Who told you this? • Where were you when you decided that? • Have you ever thought that about something you are now good at?
Everyone hates me	• What, everybody? • Who specifically hates you? • When did you decide that? • Where specifically does everybody hate you? • How do you know that?
He'll never listen	• When did you decide that? • What specifically does he not listen to? • What makes you say that? • When does he listen to you?

Exercise 1

What Meta-question could you ask in the following situations to challenge the held beliefs?

Statement	Meta-Questions
They don't like me	
Everyone hates me	
I'm not worth it	
She's always yelling at me; she doesn't like me.	

Exercise 2 - Self Coaching With Meta-Questions

1. *Write each of the following meta-questions on a separate piece of paper or card and turn them face down. Feel free to add variations of your own:*

    *   *Where specifically does this affect you?*

    *   *When specifically does this affect you?*

    *   *What impact is this having?*

    *   *When did you decide that?*

- *Who specifically does this affect?*
- *How do you know this is a problem?*
- *Where do you want this to happen?"*

2. Mix the paper or card so you do not know what is written on each.

3. Think of a problem or a challenge you would like to be coached on, (for example, improving a relationship with a family member or achieving a fitness goal)

4. Turn over one of the cards and ask yourself the question.

5. Turn over the next card and repeat the process until you have asked yourself all the questions.

Taking Meta-Questions To The Next Level

Once you are comfortable using the core five questions you can begin adding additional questions to your vocabulary. Appendix II contains an extensive list of questions.

Combining Hypnotic And Metalanguage

When used well, hypnotic language sparks our imagination. When combined with Metalanguage it can achieve truly great results. We can use Metalanguage to challenge beliefs and assumptions, then Hypnotic language to inspire change.

Consider the following examples. The negative statements are common, everyday phrases we may hear people say. The responses challenge thinking and lead the person to a more positive frame of mind:

Negative Statement	Combined Meta & Milton Responses
I'll never be any good at	<ul><li>When did you decide that?</li><li>Have you ever thought that about something you are good at?</li><li>Just imagine if you could .... Think of all the things you could achieve.</li><li>And you know you can achieve it if you put your mind to it, don't you?</li></ul>
I'll never be any good at my job.	<ul><li>What makes you say that?</li><li>How specifically does this affect you?</li><li>How could it be different?</li><li>Well, you have overcome challenges in the past, haven't you? So, you can overcome this one, can't you?</li><li>By focusing on what needs to change you will be able to achieve what you want to.</li></ul>
I'm terrified at the thought of speaking in public.	<ul><li>Where does this affect you?</li><li>What happens just before that?</li><li>How could it be different?</li><li>Imagine how good it feels when you successively speak in public. Notice the positive impact you have on others and the confidence you gain. You know you can deliver a great presentation, don't you? Have the confidence in yourself that others have in you, and you will be a great success.</li></ul>

Uncovering what's important - clean Language

The words we use can influence others in ways we didn't necessarily intend. For example, the question 'What is wrong?' is leading. It suggests something is wrong and can direct a person's thoughts towards that outcome. In contrast, a similar but open question, 'How are you?' is likely to result in a different outcome. If we can inquire without projecting our thoughts, opinions, fears, and beliefs onto others we receive more insightful responses and gain a better understanding of those we engage.

Clean Language is a set of simple questions developed by 'Counselling Psychologist' David J Grove, during the 1980s and 1990s. He noticed the clients he worked with took on the language characteristics of their therapist. He could tell which they had seen by the language they used. He believed by projecting onto their clients, therapists were less effective. The 'clean language' questions he devised allowed him to work with clients without unconsciously influencing them.

Our minds create and use imagery or metaphors to represent thoughts and feelings. These metaphors are useful in communication as they make abstract ideas more tangible. They present complex information such as our emotions, in a simple way.

Clean Language questions are powerful because they allow us to discover and use people's own metaphors. By asking clean questions, we enable people to express their own meaning, free of judgement. It promotes neutrality and objectivity in our questioning, resulting in more accurate, deeply consider responses.

Due to its simplicity and effectiveness, clean language is now widely used across multiple business sectors, including:

- Coaching and personal development
- Leadership development and motivation
- Recruitment interviews
- Sports psychology
- Agile Coaching
- Project requirement gathering
- Market research
- Business strategy development
- Counselling
- Conflict resolution.

Clean Language: Getting Started

Clean questions are incredibly simple once we are comfortable using them. Some people initially struggled as the question structure does not map nicely to the grammar we learned at school. Stick with the syntax. The questions are designed to trigger a deep level of thinking. If we change the syntax to be grammatically correct, the questions are less effective.

When setting out I suggest starting with the following three questions. You can add more as you become confident using them.

- *(And) what would you like to have happen?*
- *(And) what kind of X is that X?*
- *(And) is there anything else?*

X denotes the words/metaphors provided by the other party.

Example

A: How was your day

B: Oh, it's been hell.

A: What kind of hell is that hell?

When using clean language questions:

- Be curious and selfless. The majority of the conversation occurs in the recipient's mind, as they process the questions. We don't need to understand what is happening for the recipient for the questions to be effective.
- Listen to their words and note the metaphors in their answers. Use these to ask further clean questions.
- Ask questions in the present tense to associate the recipient into the experience.

Exercise 1 - Coaching With Clean Language

This exercise requires a willing partner who has a topic (a problem or goal) they'd appreciate some coaching on. The topic can be simple, for example, how to better manage their time, a fitness goal or where to go on holiday.

- *Ask your partner what they'd like to discuss or what's on their mind?*

- *Listen to their responses and only ask one of the three simple clean questions above.*

- *Notice their body language as they consider their answers and note the metaphors.*

- *Do this for a few minutes or until the conversation comes to a natural conclusion.*

- *After the exercise ask your partner to describe their experiences.*

* 'What would you like to have happen?' is a great question to start with (?)

The Nine Basic Clean Language Questions

Once you are comfortable asking clean language questions you can start adding more to your toolkit. The following are the nine common or basic clean questions.

- *And what would you like to have happen?*
- *And what kind of x is that?*
- *And where abouts is that?*
- *And where is that?*
- *And what happens next?*
- *And then what happens?*
- *And is there anything else?*
- *And that's like what?*
- *And where did it come from?*

Exercise 2 - Self Coaching With Clean Language

This is a simple self-coaching technique that can provide us with new insights

- *Write each of the nine clean language questions on a separate piece of paper or card and turn them face down.*

- *Mix the paper or cards so you don't know what is written on each.*

- *Think of a problem or goal you'd like to be coached on (for example, how to communicate better with a particular person in your life).*

- *Turn over one of the cards and ask yourself the question (substitute the relevant word/metaphor for x if applicable).*

- *Turn over the next card and repeat the process until you have asked yourself all the questions.*

(If your reply seems abstract, it is fine. Keep moving through the questions).

CONTROLLING THE LEVEL OF DETAIL

Have you noticed how some people really like detail? They are compelled to share every component of a story before arriving at their point. They can monopolise conversations and drag out meetings by delving into the minutiae of every topic. On the other end of the scale, some people just do not do detail. They prefer to keep conversations at a high level and struggle to focus on the specifics. We all have a natural preference. When the conversation strays from it, it can lead to tension and break rapport.

My wife is a 'detailed' person, whilst I prefer communicating at a high level. This at times has led to 'robust' discussions. The first time I dropped my kids at school I asked her what time I should set off. I expected a short response. Instead, for over five minutes, my wife explained the route she usually took and the potential obstacles I may encounter along the way. When she finally finished there was only one detail she hadn't told me, the answer to my question, the time I needed to leave?

By understanding there is a language preference for detail and how certain questions enable us to switch between the two, we can control the flow of the conversation and ensure we get what we want from it. This is also an effective tool for controlling group discussion, where a dominant individual can derail the entire meeting.

Chunking Up

If we are in a conversation that is bogged down in detail we can chunk up to a higher level by using one or more of the following questions:

- *What are we trying to achieve by doing this?*
- *What is this an example of?*
- *What is this a part of?*
- *What is the intention?*
- *For what purpose? What is the purpose of this meeting?*
- *What is the outcome we're looking for?*

Chunking Down

If we are struggling to pin someone down on specific details, imagine a politician being interviewed by a journalist, we can chunk down using one or more of the following questions:

- What/who/where specifically?
- What/*who*/*where* precisely?
- What is the evidence for that?
- *What is an example of this?*
- *What are the components of this?*

Take care when chunking between levels. We have the greatest influence when we adapt our style to that of others. Forcing our communication preference on another party can break rapport and cause conflict.

In my previous example of the school run, it was important to my wife she briefed me on the potential delays. Had she just stated a time, in her eyes she would have accepted responsibility for our children arriving at school on time. By stating all the potential challenges, she was empowering me to make the decision. A reluctance to own the decision is often the driver behind those who 'need' to provide detail. Using the questions stated earlier, I can control the level of detail in our conversations but at the expense of frustrating her. By allowing her to share the information and asking a specific follow-up question if required, both our communication preferences are satisfied.

The Art of Negotiation

The ability to help others switch between levels is a powerful negotiating tool. When talks become deadlocked, negotiators will encourage both parties to move up to a level where they agree and explore alternative options, then drill down along a different route. This approach was evident during the UK/EU trade negotiations. Each time there was an impasse and sabre-rattling from politicians, the negotiators would bring the talks back to a level of common ground. Usually "it's in all our interests to maintain a close strong, trading relationship". They would then explore alternative options before returning to the detail.

Conflict Resolution

During arguments, people tend to lose perspective and obsess over their points of view. Chunking both parties up to a point of common ground is often all it takes for people to gain a fresh perspective and a willingness to compromise. This is a technique I use frequently with my children. For example, Saturday is film night at our house. Often, peaceful family time can be delayed as the boys fight over the remote control. By chunking them up and encouraging them to remember the ultimate goal, they find common ground. In this case, they both enjoy watching films, which they aren't whilst arguing. With this new insight, the remote doesn't seem so important anymore.

Lateral chunking is equally effective in resolving workplace conflict, which in my experience, can be far pettier and more territorial than a fight over the remote control.

To move the conversation laterally we can ask questions such as:

- *What are other examples of this?*

- *What are other times you achieved this?*

- *How else can you achieve this?*

These questions enable people to think creatively or outside of the box. With new options, we can then chunk down into the detail, to define the actions.

REFRAME AND CONTROL THE NARRATIVE

"We are all in the gutter, but some of us are looking at the stars."

Oscar Wilde

Reframing is an effective way to change the direction of a conversation or unhelpful, thought processes others may have. The meaning of any experience depends on the frame around it or the context of that experience. Think of a window looking out onto a garden. If the window were moved, even slightly, the view from it would change. Reframing is essentially looking at the same situation but from a different perspective.

When we negatively perceive a situation, we focus on all that is wrong with it. We can use positive reframing to help ourselves and others change the way they think or feel about that situation. With a positive mindset, we are more likely to discover options and solutions.

Here are a few examples of reframes you might consider:

Negative frame	"My cars in the garage and won't be fixed for a week. I'll have to cycle to work."
Positive reframe	"Well, you've been saying you wanted to exercise more. You'll also be helping the environment."

Negative frame	"My boss just keeps piling up the work"
Positive reframe	"They must really trust you and believe you can do it?"
Negative frame	"My dad keeps criticising the choices I make. He treats me like a little kid."
Positive reframe	"Your dad cares about you and wants the best for you."

Reframing Questions

We can encourage others to positively reframe their experiences by asking leading questions. For examples:

- What else could this mean?
- What opportunities are there?
- Where/how could this characteristic/behaviour have a positive outcome? Where/how would it be useful?
- What would I like this to mean?

Consider the following scenarios:

Scenario 1

A parent taking their children to visit a friend.

Statement. *"The kids are too excited. They won't stop screaming and shouting."*

- What else could this mean?
- How could this behaviour be positive?

Reframe. *"It's great to see them enjoying themselves and playing together."*

Scenario 2

A broken pipe floods the kitchen, damaging the floor and work units.

Statement – *"The kitchen's ruined. Why do things like this always happen to me?"*

- What opportunities are there?
- How would it be useful?

Reframe – *"We can now re-design the kitchen and make it even better."*

Scenario 3

A friend complains they were overlooked to lead a project at work.

Statement - *"Why didn't my boss trust me to deliver this?"*

- What else could this mean?
- How could this behaviour have a positive outcome?
- What would I like this to mean?

Reframe – "They already know you are doing more than your fair share of work. They are encouraging others to step up."

Listen out for opportunities to reframe situations for yourself and others. Think about how you can turn a negative into a positive and change either your state or theirs.

WORDS WITH HIDDEN MEANING

Certain words have a hidden, subconscious meaning either for us or our audience.

But!

When we hear the word '**but**' in a sentence, it has a powerful effect. We tend to diminish the value of what has been said and place a greater emphasis on what is about to come. Consider the following sentences:

- *I can see that you are working hard, but we need more.*

- *I like hanging out with you but I'm busy right now.*

- *You look great in that but let's keep shopping and see what else we find.*

The insertion of '**but**' changes the meaning of what has been said. In contrast, consider the following sentences:

- *I can see that you are working hard. We must find a way to achieve more.*

- *I like hanging out with you. I'm really busy right now.*

- *You look great in that. Let's keep shopping in case we find something even better.*

'**Yet**' and '**however**' have a similar effect but not as powerful.

Non-Committal Language

The following words reveal our true intention: **might, may, hope to, perhaps, if I can, try, should, could, going to**.

- *I might make it tonight.*
- *I may join you if I can.*
- *I hope to be there.*
- *Perhaps we could do that.*
- *I'm going to change my eating habits.*
- *I should join a gym.*
- *I could start working out.*

How confident are you, when you hear the phrases above, that the action will be fulfilled? Not very, correct? When we use this language, not only do we sound half-hearted to those we talk to, it has a subconscious effect on us. We are telling ourselves that it is not important. When we use non-committal language, we are less motivated to fulfil the action.

Note the contrast in the following sentences:

- *I will join you tonight.*
- *I will be there.*
- *We shall do that.*
- *I've changed my eating habits.*
- *I am joining a gym.*
- *I start my first workout tomorrow.*

Why?

Take care when asking **why**, if you wish to change or disagree with the other person's opinion. Asking 'why?' subconsciously causes the recipient to search for evidence that backs up the position they hold and strengthens their point of view.

For example:

Why do you think no one likes you? What's happened to make you feel that way?

Asking 'why?' is a useful way of strengthening a point of view we like or agree with. It is used in sales to focus attention and reinforce where products are aligned to a customer's requirements. Asking questions such as "So why do you like this product? Why do you think this is a great book?" "Why do you like that feature?"

In these situations, asking why encourages the potential buyer to focus on the areas of the product that most suits their needs.

No!

This may be perceived as an abrupt and terminal response to a request or suggestion. It can trigger momentary resentment and resistance. Rejecting an idea or suggestion using other words can sound less abrasive to the other party and ensure they remain engaged for subsequent explanations.

This is particularly true for young children (and adults with low emotional intelligence), where a blunt 'no' can lead to a loud and public tantrum. Consider how the following responses sound to you:

Scenario 1 – A five-year-old child walking past an ice cream van with their parent

- "Can I have an ice cream?"

- "No. You'll be having your dinner soon".

Vs

- "Maybe later, after dinner. If you have one now, you'll not be hungry"

Both responses decline the request. Whilst the first is terminal, the second leaves the door open to the desired outcome whilst sounding reasonable.

Scenario 2 – Young employee speaking with their boss

- "Can I lead on the new account? I feel I'm ready to step up".
- "No. It's a challenging project and a tight deadline. We need an experienced hand!".

Vs

- "This is not the best account to cut your teeth on. It's challenging with difficult stakeholders. It will provide you with a great opportunity to learn and be in a great place to lead a future engagement."

Alternative responses to 'No' that soften the message include:

- Not right now
- It is not the right time
- I understand your argument. I'm doing …. because……"

"You Are Wrong!"

A statement I frequently hear in both professional and social settings. Rarely, in my experience does this statement lead to an open discussion with both parties considering the other's point of view. A direct challenge or criticism is likely to evoke defensive behaviour, potentially break rapport and damage relationships. It is also likely to entrench positions.

By challenging beliefs or opinions respectfully and positively we are more likely to encourage a constructive, robust discussion. Consider the following alternatives:

- My experience is different because.......
- I disagree because.........
- I have concerns with your approach that I'd like to discuss
- I think that .... is a better way to achieve that outcome because .....
- Have you considered ....?

Actually ...

Very similar to 'You are wrong' when used to prefix what you believe to be the correct facts, options, or opinions.

With Respect......

Again, similar to 'You are wrong'. When have you ever heard these words and felt that those delivering them were being respectful? **No offence but...**is a similar phrase.

I'm Just Saying!

The chances are if we find ourselves saying this we have just given someone some unrequested and probably unwanted, negative feedback.

To Be Honest, If I'm Honest

When we prefix a statement in this way, we are implicitly declaring that everything else we say is less than honest.

These statements can sow a seed of doubt in the minds of others.

The Power of "We"

If we wish to build relationships quickly then **We** is a powerful word. 'We' suggests part of the same group or tribe. 'We are all in this together.' It creates a common bond and implies a level of understanding. '**Us**', '**Our**', and '**Ours**' have a similar effect.

Using the words '**You**', '**Them**', and '**Their**,' may suggest difference and create subconscious barriers.

'Not' or 'Don't'

The subconscious mind cannot process negative words such as '**Not**' or '**Don't**' when they are in a sentence. For example, the statement, 'Don't think of a pink unicorn.' We must first create an internal image of a pink unicorn before we can decide to not think about it. If you don't believe me, try it.

By using these negatives in our sentences we risk embedding the very ideas that we are trying to dismiss. Considered the following:

- *Don't worry!*

- *Don't be scared!*

- *There's nothing to be scared of!*

To process the statements we must first focus on worry and being scared before we can dismiss them. And once those thoughts are in our minds, they can be difficult to reject.

These negative constructs are commonly used when communicating with children:

- *Don't do that!*

- *Don't shout!*
- *Don't run through the mud.*
- *Don't fool around.*
- *It's not playtime now!*

For a child to consider not running through the mud. They must first process the statement and imagine running through mud. So, the instruction puts the idea in their mind. When we use negative statements, we also fail to suggest the positive behaviour we want to see. Positive instructions are more likely to achieve the desired outcome. Consider the following:

- *Do this!*
- *Talk quietly!*
- *Stick to the dry parts of the path.*
- *Behave as I know you can.*
- *Let's focus when we are in the classroom.*

How about the things we tell ourselves?

- *I don't want to be unhappy anymore.*
- *I don't want to keep doing the same thing every day.*
- *It's not that I don't want to ......*
- *It's not you, it's me!*
- *I don't want to feel anxious about work.*

When I work with clients on their goals, often they are focused on what they do not want. It is only by focussing on what they want, do they have a chance of achieving it.

INFLUENCING WITH METAPHORS AND SYMBOLISM

"A story is a trick for sneaking a message into the fortified citadel of the human mind."

Jonathan Gottschall

A metaphor is a word, phrase or story describing one thing by suggesting a comparison to another, using symbolism. Our language is 'littered with metaphors. How will you **spend your time**? *Every day is a **winding road**. She is as **fit as fiddle**. He **dragged** the conversation down to **his level**.* Studies suggest we use a metaphor every 25 words. So why is it that metaphors have become such an integral part of our everyday language?

Metaphors are stories with multiple levels of meaning. They are an incredibly powerful form of communication as they influence our beliefs, attitudes, and actions on a deep level. We subconsciously process the world around us through metaphor and symbology. When we sleep, we process the events of the day, our concerns, aspirations through our dreams, which themselves are metaphors.

When we listen to a story, the conscious mind involves itself in the content, whilst the subconscious searches for similarities to real-life situations and deeper personal meaning within the context of the story.

Filmmakers, politicians, business leaders and public speakers construct metaphors to influence their audience. Well-constructed metaphors can have a profound impact on us and lead our thinking towards the underlying message of the author. You may have noticed the quotes or metaphors throughout this book, used to reinforce key points.

In 2011 a Stamford study gave two groups pamphlets on crime. The first described crime as 'a wild beast preying upon the city.' The second 'a virus plaguing the population.' When asked how to tackle crime the first group were 20% more likely to support stricter policing than the second, illustrating the impact of metaphors.

The beauty of metaphors is we all interpret them differently. We read into them our own personal experiences. If a story shows similarity to the listener's current situation, by relating to it, they can gain a different perspective and new insights.

What Makes An Impactful Metaphor?

- The story must be sufficiently different from the real-world situation otherwise we may consciously reject it.

- Elements of the story must relate to elements of the problem or situation. A team competing in the 'round the world yacht race' could be a good metaphor for a new leadership team challenged with surmounting difficult business conditions.

- Characters in the story successfully overcome challenges the listener can relate to.

- There is a sequence of events that culminate in resolving the problem or achieving the desired outcome.

Where To Use Them?

A well-crafted metaphor may be used in pretty much any situation where we would like to encourage change in others. Incorporating stories and metaphors into our conversations with friends, presentations at work or the bedtime routine with children can help challenge frustrating behaviours or inspire new personal beliefs.

The next time you notice a friend is struggling with a personal goal or limiting belief about themselves, or you need to sell an idea to your team or work colleagues, why not craft a subtle metaphor and work it into the conversation. You may be surprised by the results you see.

What Metaphors Reveal About Us

The metaphors we use to describe our world reveal a lot about who we are as they are an unconscious projection of our thoughts. When we are feeling positive our metaphors will reflect this. We may see the future as being **bright**, with **boundless opportunities**. Yet on other days, we may find ourselves on a **never-ending carousel, revisiting the same, old situation**, over and over again.

I was once asked to coach a middle management team within a large corporate organisation. I'd been informed before the session that there was building tension between the teams on the ground and the management tier. Yet when I met with the management team they described a very different situation. Their teams were working efficiently, morale was good, and it was a great place to work. Whichever question I asked, I was met with positive responses. However, one thing was amiss. The metaphors the management team used to describe this idyllic working environment were more suited to a military campaign. They talked about the need to '**choose their battles**' and '**keep their powder dry**'. How they'd created an open environment where their teams regularly '**bombarded** them with suggestions and feedback', how they felt comfortable '**defending their position**'.

After observing this incongruency between what they said and the metaphors they used for twenty minutes I challenged them on it. If everything is so positive, how come your metaphors are so confrontational? I asked. One of them responded, 'Yours would be if you worked here'. 'Really, tell me more I replied.' Within minutes a very different picture emerged. One of pent-up frustration and an 'us and them' mentality between the teams and their management.

6

DELIVER A CONVINCING ARGUMENT

"It's not what you say, but how you say it."

Mae West

How we deliver a message; the intonation, volume, and frequency, together with how we construct the sentences impacts how our words are interpreted or even whether they are heard at all. During this chapter we will explore simple rules and techniques we can all apply to our verbal communication to ensure it has a lasting impact, whether delivering the company keynote speech, working with colleagues, or conversing with friends and family.

INTONATION AND ITS IMPACT ON OTHERS

"10% of conflict is due to differences of opinion and 90% to the tone of voice"

Unknown

The voice is a remarkable instrument. An accomplished orator can deliver a speech with a music-like quality. Think of Sir Winston Churchill's delivery of his famous 'We'll fight them on the beaches' address to parliament in the build-up to the battle of Britain. Or President Obama's victory speech in 2008.

When communicating, it is the tone and intonation of our voice that clarifies and conveys the meaning behind the words. Consider the statement "I don't know". The meaning may appear obvious but depending on the context, there are numerous possibilities. It may mean "I don't care", "why are you asking me", "it's not my job", "how am I expected to know that", "I'm too busy to even think about that", "can't you work it out for yourself?" And many others including simply, I don't know. It's the tone and intonation, coupled with body language that enables us to determine the correct meaning.

Our ability to interpret and use intonation is essential to effective interpersonal communication. Most of us are pretty good at controlling the words we use, even when frustrated or annoyed. But intonation is harder to mask. I frequently work with corporate clients, helping them develop management and leadership capabilities. When a manager sounds irritated, annoyed, or disinterested whilst providing supervision it can damage morale, employee engagement and productivity as well as relationships.

CHANGE YOUR TONE AND CHANGE THE OUTCOME

By understanding our intonation and modifying it accordingly we can improve the effectiveness of what we say. Former British Prime Minister Margaret Thatcher deliberately lowered the tone of her voice to project authority in a male-dominated political world. Intonation is also important when conveying information. If we deliver information with a constant tone our audience may switch off. By varying our intonation, we are more likely to keep our audience engaged.

The most effective, deliberate use of tone I have encountered was by a former manager of mine. He had a remarkable ability to hold difficult and at times confrontational conversations without damaging relationships. When I asked how he was able to take someone to task one minute and the next return to a cordial conversation, he explained it was all down to voice tone. He confided that he never spoke to colleagues when angry. He always ensured when having a difficult conversation, he was calm and rational. Instead, he used a deliberate, stern tone to convey the seriousness of the situation. Once he said what he needed to say he would revert to his usual tone and the tension eased. This was in complete contrast to my style at the time. I hated awkward conversations. I'd put them off until I was so annoyed that my words and emotions just gushed out.

Inject Energy and Emotion

Injecting energy and emotion into our dialogue can increase engagement and empathy. This can be achieved by raising our voice and speaking in short punchy statements. When we are anxious or excited, we tend to talk quickly in short bursts as our heart rate and breathing quicken. By mimicking these physical characteristics, we can project excitement and energy into our audience.

Whilst lowering our voice, talking slowly, pausing between sentences, and holding the silence between key points encourages our audience to deeply consider and reflect upon our words.

Embrace Awkward Silences

Many of us hate an awkward silence and feel compelled to fill them with rambling words. Yet these silences can provide those we are speaking to, the opportunity to truly consider what we are saying. I've found this particularly true with new or inexperienced managers. In their one to ones with their team, they felt compelled to talk. Particularly whilst addressing negative behaviour. I encourage them to treat silence as their best friend, to make their point, then wait for the other person to speak, no matter how long it takes. The longer the silence, the more the other person has to consider their feedback.

Balanced Arguments

We are more likely to accept a statement or point of view if it is part of a balanced argument. The facts behind the argument are less important so long as the statement sounds balanced. If an argument sounds balanced we assume it is. If we wish someone to take on board our statement, provide balance.

Consider the following statements. Which sound more appealing?

"*We'll cut taxes!*" vs "*We'll cut taxes to increase growth!*"

"*We'll cut spending!*" vs "*We'll cut spending and improve efficiencies!*"

"You're not with us!" vs "*If you are not with us, you are against us!*"

The first part of a balanced statement doesn't necessarily lead to the next. In fact, the statements can be contradictory. But the fact the statements sound balanced means we are more likely to accept them at a subconscious level.

THE PERSUASION OF RHYME

Rhyme taps deep into the unconscious mind. Parents and teachers have known for years that children are more likely to believe or accept something if it rhymes. This is why rhymes are used so extensively in 'early years' education. "It's as easy as A, B, C or 1,2,3", "An apple a day keeps the doctor away." "I before E, except after C".

It's a broadly used concept in marketing. 'A Mars a day helps you work, rest and play, or "Beanz Meanz Heinz," "Once you pop, you can't stop."

Rhymes are common in political slogans. "All the way, with LBJ", "I like Ike," "Ross for boss."

And for those who can remember the highly televised OJ Simpson trial, how about, "If it doesn't fit, you must acquit."

Where a phrase or saying is judged more accurate or truthful when it rhymes is referred to as the rhyme-as-reason effect or Eaton-Rosen phenomenon. In experiments where people are asked to judge the truthfulness of statements, those that rhyme are consistently perceived more truthful than those that don't. For example, the saying "What sobriety conceals, alcohol reveals" was judged more accurate on average than: "What sobriety conceals, alcohol unmasks".

There are several theories why we believe rhyming statements to be more truthful or accurate. Firstly, because we are taught through rhyme from a highly impressionable age, by those closest to us. Consequently, we unconsciously connect rhyme with fact. Rhymes are also often repeated and passed down from generation to generation. They become embedded within family and community culture. It's also believed that rhyme enhances verbal fluency, how quickly we can cognitively process the words. The easier something is to process and recall, the more likely we are to buy into it. When you next watch television or read a magazine and notice how many straplines rhyme, give a thought to what degree you've been influenced by this.

ALLITERATION

This is where the initial sound in a word is repeated in successive words, to create a linking effect. It's also referred to as head rhyme or initial rhyme. For example, "picture perfect, "Peter Piper picked a peck of pickled peppers, "busy as a bee", "pleased as punch." As with rhyme, alliteration lends melody and rhythm to communication. It improves the fluency of words, making it easier for us to process and remember them.

REPETITION, REPETITION, REPETITION

Repetition is a fundamental part of human learning. The more we hear something, the more likely we are to remember it. Similarly, the more we hear or see a statement, the more likely we are to buy into it and believe it to be true. This is the whole philosophy behind marketing and branding campaigns. Present a product in a certain light. Associate it with athletes, celebrities or other products that support the desired image and repeat frequently.

During the Covid pandemic throughout 2020 the UK government launched a major advertising campaign to encourage people to stay home and stop the spread of the virus. The words "stay home, protect the NHS, save lives," were continually repeated across social media, poster campaigns and every political interview to huge success.

This is a technique I incorporate when working with organisations to change their culture. Ingrained beliefs are difficult to change. Tackling them head-on is likely to break rapport, damage relationships and reinforce the belief, whilst continually and subtly challenging them, chips away at them over time.

MAINTAIN A CONSISTENT MESSAGE

Some messages are harder to accept than others. Spending time preparing our audience beforehand can pay dividends. Consider how governments deliver bad news such as impending tax increases. They are likely to start preparing us before the official announcements. They will hint in interviews that something is coming; with little or no detail on what, but lots of detail on why and the benefits, *"Holes in the public finances that must be addressed to support our public services"*. By the time the official announcement is made we are expecting it and the negative impact is reduced. In contrast, positive announcements, such as tax cuts are delivered immediately to generate the biggest effect.

THREE, IT'S A MAGIC NUMBER

The human brain seems to absorb and remember information more effectively when it is presented in threes. Research suggests that an audience is more likely to consume and absorb any type of information presented to them when it is grouped in this way. That's why it's as easy as "A, B, C" or "1, 2 3". Not A, B, C, D, or 1, 2, 3 ,4. "Veni, vidi, vici". "I came, I saw, I conquered". "I came, I saw, I conquered, and returned home" does not sound right. Four examples are clearly one too many, two examples do not sound enough. Just think of all the common or memorable examples that follow the rule of three. Below are just a few.

Sport

- "On your marks, get set, go!"
- "Ready, aim, fire!"
- "Citius, Altius, Fortius!" or "Faster, Higher, Stronger!" – The Olympic Motto

Popular Culture

- Sex, drugs, and rock n roll.

- Turn on, tune in, drop out.
- "Is it a bird, is it a plane, it's superman!"
- Truth, justice, and the American way.
- Blood, sweat, and tears.
- Mind, body, and soul.

Literature

- "A horse, a horse, my kingdom for a horse!" – Shakespeare's Richard III.
- "Some are born great; some achieve greatness and others have greatness thrust upon them" – Shakespeare's Twelfth Night.
- "The ghost of Christmas Past, the ghost of Christmas present and the Ghost of Christmas Future." – Dicken's Christmas Carol.
- "Friends, Romans, Countrymen! Lend me your ears!". - Shakespeare's Julius Caesar.

Law

- "I promise to tell the truth, the whole truth and nothing but the truth".
- "I give, devise and bequeath"

Politics

- Ein Volk! Ein Reich! Ein Führer! (one nation one empire one leader)
- Life, Liberty, and the Pursuit of Happiness - U.S. Declaration of Independence

- Liberté, égalité, fraternité – The slogan of the French Republic.
- "Our priorities are Education, Education, Education" – Tony Blair.
- "Government of the people, by the people, for the people" – Abraham Lincoln's Gettysburg Address.
- "Never in the history of human endeavour has so much been owed by so many to so few" - Sir Winston Churchill acknowledgement of the RAF following the battle of Britain.
- "This is not the end. It is not even the beginning of the end. But it is, perhaps, the end of the beginning" – Also from Sir Winston Churchill's Battle of Britain speech.
- "Eat, drink and be merry, for tomorrow we may die" – French revolutionist Georges Jacques Danton.

Advertising

- "A Mars a day helps you work, rest and play" – Mars advertising slogan since 1959.
- "Stop, Look and Listen" – A UK public road and level crossing safety slogan.
- "*Beanz Meanz Heinz*" – Heinz baked beans campaign.
- 'Slip-Slop-Slap!' – Australian sun protection campaign.

So why does the rule of three work? It is down to the brain's predilection for identifying patterns. I've mentioned before that our brains are constantly searching for patterns from the data received by our senses. This is a survival strategy; it requires less conscious thinking and facilitates intuitive or instinctive behaviour. Three just happens to be the smallest number of elements required to create a pattern.

Statements that follow the rule not only sound more phonetically pleasing, they also are more likely to be remembered and to be bought into. We can use the rule of three to convey concepts more clearly, highlight points, and increase the prominence of our message. If you practice this technique, you can master it, can't you? (Did you spot how I used the rule of three?)

HUMOUR

Have you considered why we laugh at jokes and place such a high value on fun and humour? Laughter changes our brain chemistry. It releases endorphins and dopamine into the blood system. Endorphins counter Cortisol, the stress hormone. They make us feel calmer, whilst dopamine makes us feel more bonded with those around us. Humour is an important social behaviour. We use it instinctively to de-escalate tension, demonstrate we aren't adversaries and build a social bond.

Humour can be incorporated into our communication to promote togetherness and creativity or decrease stress and tension. Yet it is often underused as a communication technique. In a professional environment people incorrectly fear they may be considered unprofessional or that their message may not be taken seriously if they deliver it with humour. The evidence suggests the contrary. Studies show that leaders with a good sense of humour are perceived as nearly 30% more motivating than their counterparts. Whilst using humour in education increases the delegate's ability to learn and recall. A study undertaken in a US university showed significantly better final examination scores for a statistics course where humour had been a key factor of the learning experience.

Humour is also powerful in sales; studies show that adding a light-hearted comment to the end of a sales pitch can increase the amount people are willing to pay for a product by nearly 20%. We don't have to be seasoned comedians to gain the benefits from humour, simply being more light-hearted in our interactions with people generates similar results.

Other communication benefits of humour include:

- Our message is more likely to be remembered.
- We are perceived as more inspiring and motivational.
- It builds stronger relationships quickly.
- It encourages people to open up and talk about themselves.
- It de-escalates conflict.

THE ART OF STORYTELLING

"Culture can be defined as the stories we tell ourselves, about ourselves"

Sir Ian McKellen

Have you read an email and had to wade through paragraphs of information to decipher what the sender requires? Or been in meetings where there is lots of chatter but with no real purpose? Do you have friends who love to talk but without always having a point to make? All too often people begin communicating without considering what they wish to achieve or what they intend to say. By adopting good storytelling principles, we can create powerful messages.

For millennia storytelling has been an integral part of human culture. Passed along from one generation to the next, stories provided a vessel for important information. In an age before the written word, a tribe's heritage, the achievements and values of their ancestors, and important survival lessons were woven into stories and handed from parent to child. Those who heard them, could learn their lessons, and live longer. Over time, evolution has hardwired the need for stories into the human subconscious and they remain an incredibly powerful way to share information.

A good story told well, invokes an emotional response. As we listen to it our brain recreates the events in our mind. The subconscious mind does not differentiate between fact and fiction. Imagined events create similar brain chemistry to events experienced first-hand. This is why horror stories and films are so scary, even when logically we know there is no real danger.

By incorporating storytelling into our communication, we can convey our points in a way that our audience will relate to and remember.

The following are important factors to consider when crafting a message:

Know Your Audience

Tailor your language and style to that of your audience. What are their values and beliefs? What drives and motivates them? What level of detail do you need to go to and what language will be the most effective? How will your message impact them?

Who our story is for dictates how we should deliver it. When communicating with more than one person, decide who your primary audience is and prioritise their communication needs. A good story writer can create a tale that appeals to multiple people and groups whilst taking care that it is not at the expense of their primary audience.

Therefore, before presenting information or creating emails be clear on who it is you need to influence.

Know Your Desired Outcome

"Would you tell me, please, which way I ought to go from here?" "That depends a good deal on where you want to get to," said the Cat. "I don't much care where" said Alice. "Then it doesn't matter which way you go," said the Cat.

Alice in Wonderland - Lewis Carole

For any communication to be effective we must first be clear on the outcome we are looking for. If we do not know where we are going, how can we get there? Knowing our outcome allows us to craft a story with the appropriate underlying message. If we can't articulate what we want and why, how can we expect anyone else to figure it out?

Craft The Narrative

"I didn't have time to write a short letter, so I wrote a long one instead."

Mark Twain

Whether engaging children, talking with colleagues or presenting to the board, a well-constructed narrative can be the difference between achieving the outcome we want and not. A few points to consider:

- **What Are The Key Points?**
  Decide on the salient points beforehand that will sell the message. How can these be structured to tell an engaging story?

- **Be Concise And Succinct**
  As with any good novel or film do not wander from the script. If it is not relevant to the story, leave it out. The more concise our message, the more likely we are to retain the attention of the audience.

- **Be Clear And Specific**
  The less ambiguous our message, the more likely it is to be acted upon. Consider stating required actions upfront before presenting evidence and benefits.

- **Minimise Jargon**
  "If you can't explain it simply, you don't understand it well enough."

  Albert Einstien

  The simpler and more accessible our language, the more likely we are to win people over to our point of view. Linguistic studies show that Barak Obama's vocabulary is the simplest of any US president. Yet he is widely perceived as an intellectual, suggesting it's not the use of long or obscure words that denote intelligence but the ability to simply explain complex issues.

- **Clearly Signpost The Purpose Of Your Message**
  Would you read a book that provided no title or preview? Or watch a film not knowing what it was about? Then, why expect an audience to listen to your message or persist with a long email without a reason. Clearly stating what we want, who from, why and the derived benefits (ours and theirs) will encourage buy-in and the likelihood they will remain engaged until the end.

- **Take Care With Detail**
  Even those who have a preference for detail may not appreciate having to wade through data to identify salient points. By providing succinct summaries and access to the detail for those who want it, we engage more people.

- **Tailor Your Delivery**
  When we understand our audience, we can tailor our message to their communication preferences.

7

How To Disagree Agreeably

"Sometimes the most important conversations are the most difficult to engage in."

Jeanne Phillips

Many of us feel uncomfortable having challenging conversations or engaging with aggressive or volatile people. We tend to retreat from it. We will put up with unreasonable behaviour or compromise our views and opinions to maintain the peace.

Having the techniques and confidence to address conflict can help set boundaries and help maintain healthy relationships, significantly improve our personal well-being, and improve workplace productivity and creativity.

This chapter explores the benefits of embracing conflict, along with the practical techniques I have learnt over the past 15 years as a Team Coach, Consultant, employer, father, and husband for maintaining strong relationships whilst having difficult and challenging conversations.

EMBRACING CONFLICT

"Conflict is the primary engine of creativity and innovation. People don't learn by staring into a mirror; people learn by encountering difference".

Ronald A. Heifetz

Conflict is often quoted as a major source of workplace stress. The CBI estimates this costs UK business £4 Billion each year. Organisations are increasingly aware of the importance of employer well-being and invest in reducing workplace conflicts. However, by preventing conflict, employers are potentially suppressing the issue and reducing competitiveness.

Conflict itself is not the problem but our inability to express and resolve differences. Most of us don't like to disagree or know how to do it. We want to be liked and agreeable. We perceive disagreement as rude or unkind. It makes us uncomfortable. When others disagree with us, we can take it personally and become resentful.

Psychologists Bruce Tuckman studied the performance of teams in the workplace. He found that high performing teams experience four developmental stages, as shown in figure 7.1. For a team to become high performing it must first deal with its differences and conflicts. Yet the majority of teams never achieve this and remain in the forming stage.

Forming	Storming	Norming	Performing
- People are on their best behaviour. - Work takes place in isolation with little collaboration.	- Opinions begin to be voiced. - There is conflict and power struggles.	- Resolved disagreements and personality clashes result in stronger relationships and a spirit of cooperation.	- There is trust and transparency. - Dissent is expected and permitted so long as it supports the team's goals.

Figure 7.1 Tuckman Model of Team Development

Figure 7.2 Four Stages of Team Development

183

As a team coach, I often encountered teams of people in organisations who invest a significant proportion of their energy in maintaining the status quo. Their fear of conflict prevents them from tackling their issues and achieving their potential. One of the first things I ask them to do is embrace conflict but to do so respectfully.

Benefits Of Conflict

Below are just some of the benefits associated with positive, respectful conflict.

- **Better Solutions**
  Conflict can increase the awareness of problems and the desire to discuss them. It encourages critical examination of proposed ideas leading to better solutions.

- **Increased Productivity**
  As previously mentioned, many organisations invest a huge amount of energy in keeping the peace. Once people are comfortable having direct, robust conversations it's remarkable how much more can be achieved.

- **Greater Innovation**
  The willingness to discuss and challenge ideas leads to greater innovation.

- **Growth and Learning Opportunities**
  When our ideas are challenged we gain an opportunity to learn. Insights from others, particularly those with different experiences and outlooks can provide invaluable feedback and an opportunity to try new things.

- **Improved Relationships**
  By working through conflict, we feel closer to the people around us and gain a better understanding of what

matters to them and how they prefer to communicate or work.

UNDERSTANDING OUR ROLE IN AN ARGUMENT

"You can't change other people. You can only change yourself"

Robert HeinLein

The fact is it takes two to disagree. So before looking at techniques to challenge the negative behaviours of others it is worth examining ourselves. Is our behaviour and approach likely to resolve conflict or escalate it? The following are a few points to consider.

Controlling Our Emotions

For those of us that dislike confrontational situations, one of our biggest challenges is remaining calm and collected either during or in the build-up to the confrontation. When we are tense or stressed we are more likely to act irrationally or seek ways to avoid the confrontation.

The reality is we control our emotions. If others make us feel insignificant, small, or uncomfortable it is because we allowed them to. By no means does this condone rude or dominating behaviour but by taking charge of our own emotions we reclaim any power the aggressor has over us. For simple, practical techniques for keeping calm in stressful situations, refer to Chapter 3 'Techniques For Overcoming Anxiety and Building Confidence'.

Understand Your Triggers

There are behaviours and situations that when encountered, can trigger an unhelpful emotional response in us. This may be bullying behaviour, such as highlighting people's mistakes in public, being spoken over whilst talking or even the tone of someone's voice. The trigger can be quite unique to us. Its origin may lie deep in our subconscious, the result of childhood experiences that we've long forgotten, yet the conditioned response remains.

Consciously acknowledging these triggers and that the conditioned, emotional response is unhelpful, is the first step to changing behaviours. Again, the practical techniques in Chapter 3 can help you remain calm in stressful situations.

Change Your Perception Of Conflict

When we view conflict as negative and disagreement as rude, there is no wonder so many of us feel uncomfortable in confrontational situations. By changing how we view conflict, focussing on the benefits it can bring; an opportunity to create better solutions, personal growth, build stronger relationships to name a few, we can change how we react to it.

Set Clear Boundaries

We tend to assume that others have similar values to ours or the same ability to empathise. This is not the case. By clearly stating our boundaries, what is an acceptable way of communicating and interacting with us, early in our relationship with others, we protect ourselves whilst helping them understand the best to engage us.

Find A Quality In The Other Person You Respect

I worked on a business transformation programme with an incredibly aggressive individual. On the rare occasions people disagreed with him, he would put his hand inches from their face and tell them why they were wrong. Should they try to speak, the hand would get closer, and his voice would rise until they stopped. He was 6 ft 2" in height and his broad frame meant he towered above most people. He used his physicality at every opportunity to intimidate and bully others.

For the programme to succeed I needed to coach and influence this individual. On the surface, we had no common values. I needed a way to connect with him and see him in a positive light before I could invest my time and energy in him. So, I engaged him in conversation and asked about his interests and motivators outside of work. My view of him changed when he spoke about his family and particularly his daughters. When talking about them his hard exterior dissolved and he turned into a warm loving father. I could not coach him as a senior leader, but I could as a father.

Pick Your Battles

"Pick your battles. You don't have to show up to every argument you're invited to."

Mandy Hale

Not every disagreement warrants the time and energy to argue the case. Sometimes goodwill and compromise are of more value than being right.

How Open Are We To Other Points Of View?

"When arguing with a fool, first make sure the other person isn't doing the same thing".

Abraham Lincoln

We are all prone to overestimate our knowledge and abilities. It's known as the Dunning-Kruger effect, after the work undertaken by Psychologists David Dunning and Justin Kruger in the 1990s. Their research concluded people with limited knowledge or competence in a given intellectual or social domain greatly overestimate their own knowledge or competence in that domain relative to that of their peers.

Interestingly, once our competency in a field increases we tend to underestimate our knowledge and ability. We understand enough to know how much we don't know.

It can be helpful to keep the Dunning-Kruger effect in mind before embarking on an argument.

Using Body language To Reduce Tension

Our non-verbal communication can significantly influence the outcome of challenging conversations. Chapter 2 - How to make a great first impression, covers in detail how we can use our physiology, facial expressions, and vocal tone to project ourselves as non-threatening. Another powerful non-verbal technique is eye contact.

When we directly face someone and look them in the eye, it can trigger a stress response, particularly if we don't know them well or if we are discussing a subject likely to cause tension or disagreement. The stress response triggers our brain to produce adrenaline and cortisol. Consequently, we are more likely to make impulsive, rash decisions.

By simply focussing on something else, rather than the person we are speaking with we can prevent this instinctive stress response and de-escalate tension.

Use Props

This technique is frequently adopted within sales and consultancy. After building rapport, and instilling the virtues of their product, a salesperson will share the price. Rather than saying the price directly, they may write the price down on a piece of paper so that you are both looking at it. Should the price not land well, the conversation will continue with both parties looking at the price. This ensures the rapport that has been built up isn't broken. The salesperson and customer can then work together to overcome the problem.

I first used this technique whilst working as a consultant. When discussing the findings of a piece of work or assessment we would create a report, which we would refer to during potentially difficult conversations with the client. Our findings could be perceived as criticism. As we discussed the sensitive findings, I'd draw their attention to the report. The report was the problem, not the consultant who delivered the bad news. The client and consultant could then work together to tackle the problem report and collaborate on solutions.

It is also a handy technique for difficult workplace conversations. For example, a manager can utilise an employee's end of year report, when delivering negative feedback. Whilst discussing uncomfortable topics, they can switch attention to the report. *'John, this (the report) isn't good, is it? What are we going to do about it?'* By using the report in this way, it becomes the 'manager and employee' versus the report. Once the awkward points have been addressed, they can revert to direct communication and collaborate on the solution. The same approach works for parents tackling a negative school report.

Orchestrate The Seating

If you know you will be having a hard conversation, orchestrate the environment. Arrange the table and chairs so both parties are sat at 45° to each other, not directly opposite.

If it is a group meeting or family meal and you are expecting volatile characters orchestrate the table plan so those strongly opinionated or likely to fall out are not sitting opposite each other.

If we need to have a difficult conversation with a friend or address a child's behaviour, we can sit next to them, rather than directly in front of them.

CREATE SPACE TO THINK

When confronted with a difficult conversation, particularly if we are not expecting it, we can either over-react or retreat, implicitly agreeing with the points being made by virtue of not challenging them. I'm sure we've all experienced both these reactions and afterwards regretted not handling the conversation differently.

In an ideal world, we would have the time to reflect on what has been said and decide on the most appropriate response. We can do just that by asking buffering questions or statements. These encourage the other party to talk whilst we consider our response. Examples include:

- I understand your point of view
- Could you share your thinking on that?
- What is it you wish to achieve by...?
- I can see you feel strongly about this
- OK

As well as providing thinking time, these questions and statements show an interest in the other parties' point of view but without agreeing with it. Should we choose to, we can then challenge appropriately or at least state we disagree and why.

Choose Your Language Wisely

The language we choose can either escalate or de-escalate volatile situations. Certain words and phrases such as 'No' and 'You are wrong' are abrupt and likely to antagonise.

For non-confrontational ways to challenge see the section 'Words With Hidden Meaning'.

The Power of Names

We all respond to our name. We are programmed from birth to do so. When we hear it called we immediately pay attention. If you wish to stop someone in their tracks, use their name. You will gain their attention and an opportunity to control the conversation.

Improve Your Understanding Of Others

'Never judge another man until you have walked a mile in his moccasins'

Mary Torrans Lathrap

Perceptual positions is an NLP technique that enables us to gain insights into another person's thinking or to see a situation from multiple perspectives.

There are three perceptual positions:

First Position

It is when we talk about a situation from our point of view, through our own eyes. It is our reality. We are focused on how this situation affects us.

Second Position

This is when we adopt the other person's position. Not just what they are thinking, but also how they look and act, their behaviours, voice tonality, pitch, language etc. Imagine that you are that person and see the situation from their perspective, through their eyes.

(Note: This is a mind-read! We cannot know exactly what another person is thinking).

Third Position

From third position, we see the world from an external point of view. It is the neutral position, the fly on the wall or expert. Here we look at the first two positions with objectivity.

Exercise

- *Think of a situation where you would like a different perspective. Identify the problem scenario or relationship. It could be a family member or work colleague who you struggle to get along with or a one-off situation that has left you feeling anxious, let down or confused.*

- *Step into first position. Associate into the problem or scenario. See the situation through your own eyes.*

  o *Describe the situation in your own words.*

  o *How are you behaving?*

  o *How are you feeling?*

  o *What do you believe about the situation?*

  o *What's important to you at that moment?*

  o *What is there for you to learn?*

  o *How has your perception changed?*

- *Step into second position. Associate into the other person. See the situation through their eyes. Answer the following question as if you were them. Rather than "they did x", it's "I did x".*

  o *Describe the situation in your own words.*

  o *How are you behaving?*

  o *How are you feeling?*

  o *What do you believe about the situation?*

  o *What's important to you at that moment?*

  o *What is there for you to learn?*

  o *How has your perception changed?*

- *Step into third position. Associate into the observer/fly on the wall/expert position. Observe both parties. Again, answer the following questions as if you were them.*

  o *Describe the situation.*

  o *How are they behaving towards each other?*

  o *How do they each feel?*

o *What do they each believe about the situation?*

o *What's important to each of them?*

o *What can they each learn from this situation and each other?*

o *How has their perception changed?*

• *Return to 'First position'. Bring your new learnings and perceptions with you.*

o *How do you feel differently about the situation/problem now?*

This technique does not solve the problem. It provides greater insight into the other person's point of view. Understanding where another person is coming from, their drivers and pressures can help provide us with options for how to approach potentially difficult conversations.

GET PEOPLE SAYING YES

If we require someone's help or support, we can increase the likelihood of success by encouraging the habit beforehand. People are more likely to say yes to a big request if they have become accustomed to saying yes. So before asking for that pay rise, additional resources, or favour, start small.

Ask a series of questions that you know are likely to result in the answer 'yes'. Maybe ask for simple advice, to borrow a pen, or to be passed a cup when at the coffee machine. Once a routine or habit is formed they are more likely to support your ultimate request.

How to Give Difficult Feedback

"There is no failure. Only feedback."

Robert Allen

Feedback is an essential component of personal development. If we are not open to constructive feedback, we are closed to positive change. This section explains how we can give feedback in a way that makes it more likely to be considered and less likely to damage relationships.

Do's When Giving Feedback:

- Seek permission. If the other person is not open to feedback, it does not matter how good our delivery is. In the work context, there is often implicit permission such as one-to-ones and performance reviews. Feedback is more likely to be received well when we have explicit permission. 'Would you mind if I gave you some feedback?' is a powerful question. Once the recipient has answered 'Yes' it makes it harder for them to reject what you say.

- Avoid the 's**t sandwich' approach (compliment, criticism, compliment). People are familiar with this technique and may read it as insincere.

- Make it about behaviours, not people. Avoid personal criticism and judgement. When you .... "I felt disrespected", as opposed to "You are disrespectful", "By saying ..... in the meeting I felt you were not supporting the team", opposed to "You are not a team player."

195

- Provide evidence. This enables the recipient to consider the facts for themselves. If we cannot provide evidence when asked, we're more likely to frustrate the recipient than trigger positive change.

- Allow time for challenging feedback to be absorbed. To go straight from receiving hard feedback to a plan of action may be unrealistic.

- Frame the positive. Which is more likely to evoke positive change in you? Focussing on all your mistakes or how you can achieve future success.

- Be mindful of language. Certain words and phrases evoke a subconscious reaction. The word **'but'** causes us to diminish the value of what has just been said and heighten the value of what is to come, 'You are good at communicating with the team, but you need to improve how you are perceived by management'.

- **With respect...** When have you ever heard that said and believed it?

When Receiving Feedback

Many of us feel uncomfortable receiving compliments and quickly reject them. Consider the impact this has on the other party. They have invested their time in us, and we quickly disregard their thoughts. Whether we agree with their views or not, rejecting it or arguing why they are wrong is unlikely to change their opinion and likely to result in us receiving no more feedback. Much better to thank them for their thoughts and then decide whether we agree or not.

Managing Aggressive Behaviour

"Some cause happiness wherever they go; others whenever they go."

Oscar Wilde

Before discussing techniques, let me first clarify what I mean by difficult, aggressive, bullying, or volatile behaviour. I am sure we have all encountered people, either in the workplace, social events, or family gatherings that we struggle to connect with. People we have encountered who try to bully, dominate, or challenge us through passive aggression. I differentiate between these behaviours and violent, abusive behaviours. The later are crimes and should be treated as such. The only technique I would recommend in those situations is to extract oneself as quickly as possible from any immediate danger.

The techniques outlined in this section can be used to overcome the challenging behaviours we may encounter both professionally and socially. People generally behave the way they do because it serves them. Either consciously or subconsciously they have learnt certain behaviours are likely to achieve the outcome they desire. This section outlines the strategies I recommend for gaining a positive outcome with those we most struggle to connect with.

If you have worked through this book, you already possess knowledge and techniques to change your relationship with those you find challenging. The following is a recap of the techniques we have covered:

- Using physiology to build rapport and trust, project authority, credibility and confidence.

- Adapting our communication style to influence others.

197

- Using non-verbal communication to reduce conflict and tension.

- Using sensory acuity and eye movement to read people and understand how our message is landing.

- Using different language patterns, we can challenge strongly held views and beliefs.

- Ways to deliver difficult or challenging feedback.

- Gaining greater insight into others with perceptual positions.

The following are principles or strategies that I have found particularly useful when working and communicating with challenging people.

USE YOUR RAPPORT SKILLS

In the section 'How to Make A Great First Impression', we looked at how we can build rapport or trust through our non-verbal communication. The following are practical techniques where rapport may be used to change challenging or aggressive behaviours in others.

Pace And Lead To A More Helpful State

When we engage someone who is feeling angry or frustrated, telling them to calm down is likely to have the opposite effect. It is also likely to break rapport, as our calm physiology, tone and volume are unlikely to match theirs. Matching their physiology and tone, though slightly less intensely, will build rapport. From there we can pace and lead them to a calmer place. Read the section on 'Building Rapport Or Trust' to familiarise yourself with how to pace and lead.

Deliberately Break Rapport

"You can catch more flies with honey than with vinegar"

Benjamin Franklin

Deliberately breaking rapport can be an effective technique to counter aggressive, dominating, or unreasonable behaviour. By demonstrating polar opposite behaviours, becoming 'reasonableness personified' through the exchange, remaining calm but firm, meeting accusations with considered responses, whilst maintaining confident physicality, aggressors will likely tire.

They are also likely to become self-conscious, particularly if the exchange is in earshot of others. Generally, people know when their behaviour is unacceptable, but justify it by the outcome. *"The end justifies the means!"*. The longer the exchange goes on, the more uncomfortable they become. We can intensify that discomfort by calmly and politely asking questions such as, "Are you aware you are shouting right now?" "Could you please stop shouting at me?" "Would you like me to come back later when you've had a chance to calm down"?

8

GROUP MENTALITY

"Coming together is a beginning, staying together is progress, and working together is success."

Henry Ford

Our ability to engage, challenge and influence diverse groups is increasingly important. Continued marketplace globalisation, geopolitical hotspots, and environmental challenges such as climate change all require a concerted international response. Whilst the need for effective communication and collaboration has never been stronger, the larger and more disparate the audience the greater the chance of miscommunication and misunderstanding.

This chapter has been specifically written for those who work with or lead teams of people. We will examine why human behaviour differs within groups compared to one-to-one conversations, the challenges this creates, and ways to avoid or overcome these challenges.

CROWD PSYCHOLOGY

"Collective fear stimulates herd instinct, and tends to produce ferocity toward those who are not regarded as members of the herd."

Bertrand Russell

How we react and behave can vary greatly depending upon who we are with. Studies show that individuals will modify their opinions and compromise their values to conform to group norms. These modifications can be quite pronounced depending on the size of the group and the personalities within it.

Social psychologists believe this desire to conform is due to the essential benefits we gain from being part of a group. Throughout history, we have relied on groups or tribes for protection against predators and rivals, to acquire and protect resources and to support each other through hardship. To be without a tribe was likely to have dire, if not fatal, consequences.

Today group and social interactions are still important. Our communities give us purpose. They protect us from loneliness and provide us with support and encouragement. By conforming we demonstrate our willingness to be a part of the group, increasing the likelihood the group will be there for us in return.

Group conformity can be a positive force if the group supports positive behaviours. Working as teams, we can achieve more, leverage collective skills and experiences and we can learn from each other. But group mentality or group thinking can also silence criticism and dissent, it can prevent individuals from exploring ideas outside of those preferred by the group and it can elevate dominant group members' opinions above the rest.

Our conformity impulse is so strong it can overwhelm our better judgment. At its most extreme, behaviours can be amplified, and individuals can behave out of character and in ways they later regret. This is evidenced in examples of social unrest, riots, and looting, where protests may begin peacefully but quickly turn ugly. Many who subsequently break the law are caught up in the group and can act quite out of character.

A series of experiments undertaken by psychologist Solomon Asch in the 1950s illustrated the degree to which an individual's beliefs and opinions could be altered by group thinking. One famous experiment placed eight participants in a group and asked each member to decide which of three, different sized lines was the same length as a fourth line. The answer was obvious, but the experiment wasn't what it seemed. Seven group members were actors who had been instructed to give incorrect answers, unbeknownst to the eighth member of the group. Faced with either going against the group or conforming, approximately 75% of test subjects agreed with the wrong answer at least once during the experiment.

By understanding and accepting 'Crowd Psychology' we are better placed to structure and tailor our communication to achieve the best outcome.

COMMUNICATION FACTORS TO CONSIDER

The following are the key factors to consider when engaging groups of people.

Communicate The Right Information

Many organisations I work with value openness and transparency. They use monthly town halls or company-wide announcements to share the views of the senior leadership team and provide updates on performance figures. Engaging everyone at the same time they believe promotes inclusive decision-making and company buy-in. They are surprised when employee surveys consistently show communication, transparency and empowerment are concerns for their workforce.

Although their communication strategy is well-meant, it is not what their employees wanted and didn't provide them with a safe space to challenge or raise concerns. Before scheduling a company-wide 'town hall', group workshop or meeting consider:

- **The Needs Of Your Audience** - What is it they want and expect? If we don't know the answer, undertake research. Engage with smaller groups and individuals. Conduct employee surveys and be curious. Otherwise, not only may we lose an opportunity to inspire and motivate, we are likely to waste their time and breed resentment.

- **Your Desired Outcome** - All too often organisational communication occurs because leaders feel it is expected, rather than there being a specific outcome in mind. If it is unclear what we wish to achieve, it's unlikely we'll achieve it. Often the driver is vague employee feedback referencing communication. This can lead to more rather than better or tailored communication.

- **Who To Include** - Meetings and large gatherings provide an opportunity to communicate a consistent message to multiple people. But the larger the gathering, the harder it is to manage the message. It may be easier and more effective to hold multiple smaller sessions or key one-to-one sessions.

- **Don't Over-Communicate** – Over-communication can cause as many problems as under-communication. When too much information is shared, the important information may be lost in the noise. Many organisations feel the need to over-communicate. Particularly if employee feedback has highlighted communication as an issue. It is generally assumed that more communication, rather than better or even less, will resolve the problem.

Build Rapport Through Words And Physiology

It is harder to build rapport with a group than with individuals, as group members are likely to behave and act differently to each other. We can still use the rapport techniques covered in chapter 2, including:

- Project confidence, authority and likeability using physiology. Use open hand gestures and inclusive language.

- Mirror, matching and crossover matching. It is impossible to do so with everyone in the audience but if we can identify the leaders or dominant personalities and build rapport with them, we are likely to take the rest with us.

- Identify common ground. Demonstrating we hold the same values and interests as our audience builds trust. Gaining trust is essential before moving on to challenging topics.

Communication Preferences

We discussed in chapter 4, communication preferences. How each of us has a preferred communication style and the best way to inspire, motivate and influence others is to adapt our style to match theirs. When speaking with a group, there is likely to be multiple communication preferences present. Therefore, it is not possible to match each simultaneously. We can appeal to as many preferences as possible by varying the predicates we use. See predicate words in chapter 4. Also, by keeping communication at a high level but making detail available for those who need it, we are more likely to connect with the majority of the audience.

Multiple Channels And Consistent Messaging

Not everyone interacts with information in the same way. To achieve the best outcome, utilise a variety of communication channels. Consider political or public health campaigns. They use multiple channels: television, social media, posters, podcasts, and interviews to convey their message. They also repeat the message. We are inundated by thousands of messages each day, adverts, memes, posts. By continually repeating the same, consistent message it is more likely to stand out and be remembered.

This approach was evident during the global covid pandemic. Governments around the world used multiple communication channels to deliver a complex set of public health guidelines. Great effort was made to deliver the message simply and consistently. Occasionally a public official or politician would go off script and suggest a scenario contrary to the agreed narrative, which caused confusion, led to public anxiety, and consumed valuable airtime for others to retract the comments.

I frequently work with multinational corporations that are implementing large scale business transformation programmes. Typically, these programmes change the organisational structures, business processes and the jobs that people do. It can be an unsettling time for those affected. Ensuring consistent, clear, and relevant communication occurs when required, is essential to success. When organisations get this wrong, a huge amount of time, money and employee goodwill can be wasted attempting to rein in unhelpful and inaccurate versions of events.

Seek Out Feedback

"In teamwork, silence isn't golden, it's deadly"

Mark Sanborn

Feedback is critical to successful communication. If we are unaware of how our message landed, how do we know whether what we said was understood as intended? We covered the importance of feedback for effective communication in Chapter 1, 'The Science Of Communication'.

Many of us find it a challenge to get feedback in a one-to-one scenario, so how can we achieve it whilst communicating with a group? The following are a few simple techniques I use.

- **Be Receptive** – When requesting feedback be ready to hear it and act upon it. Otherwise, why should people waste time providing it?

- **Body Language** – When addressing a group, it isn't possible to closely observe people's facial expressions and body language. They may be too far away or joining remotely. We can often observe a few tell-tale signs. If the group occasionally nods or smiles at our points, it's a good sign they are on board. If it's a large and important gathering I often ask others if they would observe the group for me. So, whilst I'm focussed on delivering the message, they can identify anyone who may have had concerns. That way I can follow up with those people at a more appropriate time.

- **Real-Time Questions** – Providing a tool for people to raise questions or express their thoughts during large gatherings is a popular technique used by many organisations, to provide everyone with a voice. The comments may be anonymous to reassure those taking part. It can be a little nerve-wracking for those at the front. I've given talks at public events where these tools are used and received a few challenging questions. Nevertheless, they are an effective way for large groups to collaborate.

- **Check-In** – Arranging follow-up sessions after a large cascade of information, whether smaller meetings with line managers or tailored surveys, can provide an opportunity for the group to ask questions once they've had a chance to digest the information.

Business Meetings

I could not write this book without mentioning meetings. If there is one thing I find universally loathed by the organisations I have worked with, it is excessive and unproductive meetings. Most of the workplace meetings I have attended fall into one of those two categories.

There is no disputing the need for colleagues to meet so they can cooperate and collaborate. Yet many of the meetings organisations hold can prevent this from happening. The available data around meetings is quite shocking.

Figure 8.1

The online scheduling service, Doodle, studied over 6,500 people in the US, UK, and Germany, and analysed over 19 million meetings. They estimated inefficient meetings cost US businesses $399 billion and UK $58 billion during 2019. Whilst surveys by the HR Digest suggest between 30% to 50% of our time spent in meetings is unproductive.

So why do so many organisations get it wrong?

Causes Of Unproductive Meetings

Preparation

"If You Fail to Plan, You Are Planning to Fail"

Benjamin Franklin

Often when working with organisations I will arrive at a meeting where there has been zero planning. There's no agenda or idea of how the session will be run. In response to a problem, a meeting was scheduled, and any relevant party invited. The attendees are then supposed to take it from there.

My advice for organisations when running meetings, workshops or group sessions is before scheduling it, plan:

- What is the outcome you want to achieve?
- How will you achieve it? (What's the meeting structure or agenda)
- Who should attend? The larger the number the harder the session will be to run.
- Do attendees need to prepare? If so, what is expected of them.

- What do the attendees want from the session?
- What questions are likely to be asked?

If the correct level of preparation has not taken place, the likelihood is, it will be an unproductive session. The most effective way to positively change poor meeting culture is to empower people to reject an invite or to leave a meeting if the correct level of planning and preparation has not occurred.

Invite The Right People

The larger the meeting, the harder it becomes to facilitate. Yet when I work with organisations I often see meetings and brainstorming sessions attended by more than 30 people. It is physically impossible for any facilitator to ensure that number of people have an equal voice. I find a good rule of thumb when running meetings is, if the attendee list grows above 10, cascade information instead.

The need to invite everyone usually stems from one of the following:

- Habit. Probably the biggest cause of unnecessary meetings. If there is a problem, call a meeting.
- Collective decision making. When leaders lack the confidence to make decisions, meetings can provide a way of sharing that responsibility and diluting accountability.
- The organiser either didn't understand the issue or hadn't the time to analyse it. So, they invited everyone who may have a view.
- The organiser doesn't see running the session or the outcome as their responsibility, only ensuring it's in the calendar.

- Internal politics dictate who should be represented, with people attending to 'protect their area'.

Sensitivity Of The Topic

"Praise in public, criticise in private"

Vince Lombardi (NLF Coach)

Delivering sensitive, critical, or bad news in an open forum without prior warning is likely to trigger defensive behaviour. Much better to address concerns on a respectful one-to-one basis than in a public forum. I have witnessed leaders publicly criticise staff. Or demand to know "Who's at fault." I am yet to see this approach solve any problem. It only creates resentment from those involved and mistrust from those who witnessed it.

PSYCHOLOGICAL SAFETY

"The best single question for testing an organisation's character is: What happens when people make mistakes?"

Robert Sutton

Not everyone is comfortable sharing in a group discussion. Many find it quite terrifying. Creating psychological safety, a space where all may share without fear of negative consequences is essential to gain the most from a group.

Tips To Achieve Psychological Safety

- **Lead by example and with empathy**. Tackle bad behaviour immediately regardless of where it comes from.

Organisational culture is determined by the worse behaviours the leaders are prepared to tolerate.

- **Ensure everyone has a voice**. Be observant. Note who shares ideas and who doesn't. Encourage the quiet ones to find their voice.

- **Be open and embrace feedback**. If we are not prepared to accept feedback from those around us, what gives us the right to critique their work? You may find that by embracing feedback yourself you inspire others to do the same.

- **Invest in relationships**. Be curious and actively listen. Endeavour to understand the individual goals and personal drivers of the group or team, so you can help them accomplish them.

- **Promote learning not a fear of failure**. If people are constantly looking over their shoulder, fearing the ramifications of making a mistake, they are unlikely to reach their full potential. As learning new skills and trying new things involves risk and we don't always get it the right first time. All the brilliant people I have worked with agree that they have learnt far more from their failures than they did their successes.

9

TAKING YOUR SKILLS TO THE NEXT LEVEL

"Knowledge is of no value unless you put it into practice."

Anton Chekhov

Having read this book, you now have a solid understanding of human communication along with great verbal and non-verbal techniques. You understand:

- Why human communication can break down.
- How to use your physiology to build rapport and trust, project authority, credibility, and confidence.
- The importance of communication preference, and your own personal preferences.
- How to influence others by adapting your communication style to match theirs.
- How to use your physiology to reduce conflict and tension.
- How sensory acuity and eye movements provide an insight into what others are thinking.
- How using different language patterns, you can challenge strongly held views and beliefs, gain insights, build confidence and self-belief, influence and inspire.
- How to effectively deliver challenging feedback without damaging relationships.
- How to gain greater insight into other people through perceptual positions.

This chapter outlines how we can continue to improve our communication skills and further develop the techniques we have learnt.

STAGES OF LEARNING

When mastering new skills, it is helpful to understand how we learn. The Conscious Competence Ladder (Figure 9.1) developed by Noel Burch explains the factors that affect learning.

Unconsciously Competent	Unconsciously Incompetent
Consciously Competent	Consciously Incompenet

Figure 9.1 Noel Burch's Conscious Competence Ladder

Stage 1. Unconscious Incompetence

This is when we are unaware of how to undertake a particular skill, or even that the skills exist. Before we can progress to the next stage of learning we must accept our competency and have the desire to improve. Most of us are unable to drive a car until we have lessons. Up until the legal age of driving, most people probably gave little thought to the 'skills required'. They were unconsciously incompetent. Once an individual decides they want to drive, the first step is usually to take lessons.

Stage 2. Conscious Incompetence

This is when we are aware that we can't perform a particular skill or lack certain knowledge and expertise. We can acquire the skills and/or knowledge through training and experience.

Stage 3. Conscious Competence

Through learning and experience, a point will come where we understand or know how to do something. However, demonstrating the skill or knowledge requires concentration.

Stage 4. Unconscious Competence

This is when we have acquired so much experience performing an activity that it has become "second nature". We do not need to think about it to do it. If you can ride a bike, cast your mind back to when you first began learning. You probably had to focus really hard on what you were doing and the process you had to follow. Now you can ride a bike, it is unlikely you still follow those steps. You just do it without giving it a great deal of thought.

When you decided to pick up this book, the chances are you were moving from stage 1 to 2. You had become conscious there were certain areas of your communication you would like to improve. Through reading this book and practising the techniques you can transition from Stage 2 to Stage 3. You will be consciously able to use the skills you have learnt and gain positive results. By continually practising, over time you will hone your skills, that they become second nature. You will perform them without thinking. You will become unconsciously competent.

The Key To Mastering Communication Skills

The key to mastering any skill is simple. Practice, practice, practice.

The more we practice the better we become. By continually repeating any activity, over time we create new habits. If we practice one technique frequently such as sensory acuity or reading eye pattern movements, after a few weeks our proficiency will improve, and the activity will become a subconscious behaviour. We will do it naturally, without thinking about it.

I recommend you identify a few techniques that appeal to you or that you believe will have the greatest benefit. Practice them until they become second nature. Then add more to your repertoire.

GLOSSARY

Auditory	The representational system for hearing.
Auditory Digital	The representational system for logic and how we talk to ourselves.
Beliefs	Subjective ideas or generalisations about what is true and not true for ourselves and the world.
Calibration	The ability to notice and measure change compared with a baseline. Usually involves the comparison between two different sets of external non-verbal cues for a particular person such as facial expressions and eye pattern movements.
Chunking	A process of changing perception by moving a person's thinking in the direction of more abstraction, more detail or laterally.
Clean Language	A technique originally used in counselling, psychotherapy and coaching but now also used in education, business, organisational change, and health. It allows someone to explore their own reasoning without being influenced by those asking the questions.
Clean Questions	Questions that allow the recipient to draw their own conclusions without influence from the questioner.
Communication Model	A model of how people internally process external events and how this

internal processing impacts on behaviours and results.

Cross-over Matching Matching one aspect of a person's external behaviour or physiology with a different physiological movement.

Deletion Occurs when we leave out a portion of our experience as we make our internal representations.

Distortion Occurs when something is mistaken for that which it is not, or when things that have not occurred are included in our internal representations.

Double Bind Questions that provide the illusion of choice. Two options, each leading to the desired outcome of the author.

Filters What determines the categories of information that is cognitively processed or rejected.

First Position One of the perceptual positions. From first position, you see things from your personal point of view.

Embedded Command A command within a longer sentence, marked out by voice tone or gesture.

Embedded Question A question within a longer sentence, marked out by voice tone or gesture.

Eye Accessing Cues Movements of the eyes in certain directions indicating access to visual, auditory, kinaesthetic, or auditory digital modes of thinking.

Generalisation	Occurs when one specific experience is used to represent a whole class of experiences.
Gustatory	The representational system for taste.
Hierarchy of Ideas	The level of abstraction of ideas and concepts, ranging from abstract to specific.
Internal Representations	The content of our thinking which includes pictures, sounds, feelings, tastes, smells, and self-talk. It is how we perceive the external world and our imagined experiences.
Kinaesthetic	The representational system for feelings and sensations.
Lead System	See preferred representational system.
Linguistic Presupposition	The subconscious assumptions we make to construct or understand sentences.
Matching	Copying to some degree, one or more aspects of a person's physiology or voice.
Metaphor	A metaphor is a figure of speech that directly refers to one thing by mentioning another.
Meta Model	A model of language, derived from the work of Virginia Satir. It allows us to recognise the deletions, generalisations and distortions in our language and

gives us questions to clarify imprecise language and specificity.

Meta Programs Unconscious programs we run that filter our experiences.

Milton Model A set of language patterns used by Milton Erickson to create trance or agreement. The language is purposefully ambiguous so that people can create their own meaning.

Mirroring Reflecting the physiology of someone as if looking into a mirror.

Olfactory The representational system for smell.

Pacing Gaining and maintaining rapport with another person by matching or mirroring their external behaviours.

Perceptual Positions Describes our point of view from different positions. Enables us to get an insight into other peoples' perceptions.

Predicates Words and phrases that often presuppose one of the representational systems.

Preferred Representational System The representational system that someone most often uses to organise their experiences. This is the representational system that we most commonly and easily deploy.

Presuppositions The assumptions people make to support their model of the world. They provide an insight into our belief system.

Rapport   The ability to relate to others and build trust and understanding.

Reframing   Viewing a problem or situation from a different perspective.

Second Position   Relates to perceptual positions. Second position is the view from the other person's position.

Sensory Acuity   The ability to notice and gain awareness of another person's conscious and subconscious responses through their physiology or voice.

State   Our internal emotional condition.

Third Position   Relating to perceptual positions. The third position is the view of the observer.

Trance   An altered state whereby an individual's attention shifts from their external to their internal reality.

Values   Attributes that are important to you or that you look for or want in something.

Visual   The representational system for sight.

APPENDICES

I. Communication Preference Questionnaire

To determine your personal communication preferences, answer the following questions and enter the values in the subsequent tables.

Step 1
Score each of the seven questions with a value according to the list below:

4 = Most accurate

3 = Second most accurate

2 = Third most accurate

1 = Least accurate

1. When considering a holiday, place the following in order of appeal:
    _____ The feel of the hot sand underfoot and the warm breeze on my face.
    _____ The gentle sound of lapping waves and songful birds in the distance.
    _____ Knowing the resort has good reviews and star ratings.
    _____ The beautiful shorelines, bright blues sky, and the turquoise water.

2. I approach problems by:
    _____ Studying the options and formulating a plan in my head.
    _____ Stepping back and getting a grasp on what is needed.
    _____ Looking at the bigger picture to see the solution.
    _____ Listening to the arguments and going with what sounds right.

3. I work at my best when:

_____ I have a clear picture of the way forward.

_____ I have a firm handle on what is needed.

_____ I have a good understanding of what is required.

_____ The instructions are loud and clear.

4. When buying a new car, I make my decision based on:

_____ The specifications, mileage, safety features and purchase price.

_____ The colour, styling and how I would look driving it.

_____ The purr of the engine, quality of the sound system and whether it sounds like good value.

_____ How comfortable it is to drive and if it feels like a good deal.

5. During a presentation or debate, I am most often influenced by:

_____ The presenter's logic and how they structure their argument.

_____ How they vary their tone of voice to project their points and the words they say.

_____ Building a picture of their story and whether I can see their point of view.

_____ The energy and passion of the presenter.

6. One of my strengths is my ability to:

_____ Quickly tune in to what is important.

_____ See what needs to be done.

_____ Quickly get a feeling for what matters.

_____ Make sense of new facts and figures.

7. When you agree with an idea you are more likely to say:

_____ That looks right.

_____ That makes sense.

_____ That sounds right.

_____ That feels right.

Step Two

Copy the sequence of values from each question to the table.

Q1		Q2		Q3		Q4		Q5		Q6		Q7	
	K		AD		V		AD		AD		A		V
	A		K		K		V		A		V		AD
	AD		V		AD		A		V		K		A
	V		A		A		K		K		AD		K

Step Three

Transfer the score associated with the letters V, A, AD and K, for each question, to the table below. There will be seven entries per letter.

Question	V	A	AD	K
1				
2				
3				
4				
5				
6				
7				
Totals				

The final totals are your preferred Primary Representational System: (at the time you completed the questions)

II. HYPNOTIC LANGUAGE

The following is an extensive list of hypnotic language patterns. Do not be put off by the complex, official labels. You do not need to know or understand the label to use the language pattern.

Distortions

Mind Read

Claiming to know what someone is thinking gives credence to the next part of the sentence.

- I know that you are wondering ..... just how good my other programmes are.

- I see you are curious ...... about just what you will achieve by mastering these language patterns.

Lost Performative

Judgement without stating who is judging.

The subconscious accepts the statement without questioning the authority.

- And it is good to wonder *(according to who?)* ...... just how good you can become.

- It is great to invest in yourself.... by learning these language patterns, you will be able to connect with so many more people.

- That is right.

Cause And Effect

Implying one thing leads to another. If.... then...   As you..... then you

- If you practice a language pattern every day, in no time at all you will become proficient.

- By studying, you will learn all you need to know about language patterns.

- As you consider just how much you have learnt on this programme then you appreciate just what a good communicator you have become

Complex Equivalent
When one thing equals another

- The more you study, the more you learn.

- Because you invest in your personal development you are becoming a better person

Standard Proposition
Talking about the consequence of something whilst avoiding the cause

- You are learning new ways to effectively communicate.

- Have you noticed just how easily you can learn new skills?

Generalisations

Universal Qualifier
Generalisations that do not specify what or who you are referring to. They contain the words 'all', 'every', 'never', 'always', 'nobody'.

- Every single one of us can change.

- You will relax more with every breath that you take.

- We are all in this together.

Model Operators Of Possibility Or Necessity

Statements that imply possibility or necessity. You can use these statements to loosen people's thinking. They contain words such as 'will', 'can', 'may', 'must', 'should', 'need'.

- You can achieve whatever you want to, with dedication.

- We must seize the opportunities we have.

- You will become a brilliant communicator if you practice these language patterns.

Deletions

Unspecified Verbs

Verbs that do not specify the action taken. The listener is forced to supply the meaning.

- You can do this, can't you?

- It's easy, isn't it?

Simple Deletions

Where the object, person or process of the sentence is missing.

- With time you'll understand

- As you wonder

Lack Of A Referential Index

The subject of the sentence is missing. Recognised by the words it, them, that, thing, stuff, people, one, others.

- One can, you know, learn language patterns easily.

- People always surprise us.

- Others will notice the difference when you begin using these language patterns.

Comparative Deletion

When a comparison is made without specifying what it is being compared to. Yet the subconscious still accepts the comparison.

- It is the same thing, more or less.

- Things are much better now.

- We all know that feeling.

Further Hypnotic Patterns

Embedded Commands

Instructions embedded in a sentence that direct someone to do something. They tend to have a double meaning. One for the conscious mind and another for the subconscious. The subconscious has to consider the instruction to process it.

- You, like me, are passionate about personal development.

- People who trust me are a good judge of character.

Embedded Questions

A sentence within a question where no overt response is expected.

- I wonder who within the group will master language patterns first?

Tag Question
A question tagged to the end of a statement designed to remove resistance to the statement.

- You can, can't you?
- I can see you will make that change, won't you?
- By practising hypnotic language you'll be able to influence those around you, won't you?
- You are getting these language patterns now, aren't you?

Double Bind
Providing the illustration of free choice whilst leading the recipient along a predetermined path.

- Will you have a bath before or after storytime?
- Would you like to eat Italian or Thai?
- Will you send me the report today or tomorrow?

III. META-QUESTIONS

The following is an extensive list of meta-questions. Do not be put off by the complex, official labels. You do not need to know or understand the label to use the language pattern.

Examples Of Deletions

Meta Pattern	Possible Responses	Predicted Outcome
Nominalisations: Turns verbs into nouns. "There is no understanding here." In this context 'understanding' has greater meaning than the dictionary definition.	"Who is not understanding whom?" "How would you like to understand?" "Has there been a time when there was understanding?" "When did you decide that?"	Recovers the deleted referential index (The person or thing that is referenced). The meaning of 'understanding' is recalculated. The additional information provides options.
Unspecified Verbs No subject information provided. "They rejected me." (Who did?)	"How specifically did they reject you?"	Specifies the verb. Re-evaluates 'rejected'.

Simple Deletions The subject is missing. "I am very unhappy." (About what?)	"About what/who specifically?"	Recovers the deleted information.
Lack of Referential Index Failure to specify the person or thing. "Everyone thinks I'm stupid." (Who is everyone?)	"Who specifically thinks you are slow?" "What everyone?"	Recovers the index and enables the conclusion to be challenged.
Comparative Deletions What it is being compared to has been deleted. "That's too expensive."	"Compared to what/who?"	Recovers the comparison deletion and challenges the conclusion

Examples Of Distortions

Meta Pattern	Possible Responses	Predicted Outcome
Mind Reading: Claiming to know what others are thinking. "I know they hate me."	"How specifically do you know?"	Recovers the source of the information and challenges the conclusion.
Lost Performative Value judgments where the person judging is left out. "It's wrong to feel this way."	"Who says it's wrong?" "According to whom?" "How do you know it's wrong?" "When did you decide that?"	Gathers evidence, recovers the source of the belief, and challenges it.
Cause And Effect Where Cause is incorrectly assigned to someone else. "You ruin everything for me."	"How specifically do I ruin everything?" "How do my actions make you feel that way?"	Recovers choice. Challenges the causality.

Complex Equivalence		
Where two experiences are assumed connected. "They are always screaming at me. They hate me".	"How does them screaming at you mean they hate you?" "Have you never screamed at someone you like?" "When did you decide that?"	Recovers the complex equivalent so it may be challenged.
Presuppositions Assumed facts in a statement. "If she knew how hard I've tried she wouldn't say that?"	"How do you know she doesn't know?" "What specifically is she doing?"	Recovers information about the presupposition so it may be perceived differently.

Examples Of Generalisations

Meta Pattern	Possible Responses	Predicted Outcome
Universal Quantifiers These are large generalisations. Denoted by the words: all, never, everyone. "Everybody hates me."	"What, everybody?" "Is there anyone that doesn't hate you?" "When did you decide that?"	Recovers information about the generalisation and challenges the belief.

Modal Operator Of Necessity These illustrate the rules in our lives. Denoted by the words should, must, ought to. "I must get this done tonight."	"What would happen if you did/didn't?" "What wouldn't happen if you did/didn't?"	Recovers the effects and outcomes. Enables conclusions to be reconsidered.
Modal Operator Of Possibility These illustrate what we believe is possible. Denoted by the words may/may not, can/can't, will/won't, possible/impossible. "I can't tell him the truth."	"What's stopping you?" "What would happen if you did/didn't?" "What wouldn't happen if you did/didn't?"	Recovers causes. Enables re-evaluations.

IV. Clean Language Questions

The following is an extensive but by no means exhaustive list of clean questions.

Developing questions encourages the recipient to think more deeply, to create imagery and metaphors that express their thoughts and feelings.

Moving In Time questions. These allow the recipient to gain the perspective of time. To explore how they have succeeded in the past or view the current situation from a future perspective.

Note: X and Y denote the words/metaphors provided by the other party.

Developing Questions

(And) what would you like to have happen?

(And) what kind of X (is that X)?

(And) is there anything else?

(And) is there anything else about X?

(And) where is X?

(And) that's like what?

(And) is there a relationship between X and Y

Moving In Time (Sequence Or Strategy) Questions

(And) then what happens? Or (And) what happens next?

(And) when X, what happens to y?

(And) what happens just before X?

(And) where could X come from?

Intention Questions

*X can be replaced by "You" in the first instance

(And) what would X like to have happen?

(And) what needs to happen for X?

(And) can X happen?

ACKNOWLEDGEMENTS

My students and clients whose desire to learn and improve have been a constant inspiration.

Richard Bandler and John Grinder for being curious about human excellence and their modelling work with Virginia Satir, Milton Erickson and Fritz Perls.

David Grove and Caitlin Walker for their work on clean language and symbolic modelling.

Michael Grinder for his techniques on non-verbal communication.

Mark Bowden for his inspirational body language talks and demonstrations.

Dale Carnegie for writing the book that inspired me to change, and my friends at Dale Carnegie Training for challenging me to be a better coach and trainer.

Steve Adams, Toby and Kate McCartney for their training, mentoring and guidance.

Printed in Great Britain
by Amazon

38575979R00139